Frank Power

Letters from Khartoum

written during the siege

Frank Power

Letters from Khartoum
written during the siege

ISBN/EAN: 9783742875372

Manufactured in Europe, USA, Canada, Australia, Japa

Cover: Foto ©ninafisch / pixelio.de

Manufactured and distributed by brebook publishing software (www.brebook.com)

Frank Power

Letters from Khartoum

LETTERS FROM KHARTOUM

WRITTEN DURING THE SIEGE

BY THE LATE
FRANK POWER
H.B.M.'S ACTING-CONSUL; CORRESPONDENT FOR THE "TIMES," ETC. ETC.

LONDON
SAMPSON LOW, MARSTON, SEARLE & RIVINGTON
CROWN BUILDINGS, 188 FLEET STREET
1885
[*All rights reserved*]

PREFACE.

I HAVE been induced to publish the following letters, not from any idea of their literary merit—they pretend to none—but because I feel certain that every Englishman at this moment is anxious to receive any items of information that can be gleaned about General Gordon and his gallant defence of Khartoum.

An account, however hastily written, and comprising however short a period, when given by one who was present and saw what things were done; who shared the dangers of the siege with England's latest hero and his brave lieutenant, Colonel Stewart; who enjoyed Gordon's confidence, and who was capable of understanding and appreciating what he saw, should surely be of great interest to every one. These conditions the account contained in my brother's letters fulfil. He was in Khartoum from the 1st August, 1883, until the 10th September, 1884, and, as stated in a recent article in the *Times*, "it was almost exclusively through Mr. Power's despatches that England and Europe first of all learnt of the disaster which befell Hicks Pacha's army, the triumph of the Mahdi, and the gradual closing of the enemy around Khartoum. Afterwards it was from him we had the graphic and stirring accounts of General Gordon's arrival, of his energetic efforts to establish order and to keep the hostile tribes around him at bay; of his victories and his misfortunes; of the valour of his Bedouin foes, and the treachery and cowardice of his Turkish and Egyptian troops." And, again, after nearly half a year's silence (and what message could tell of the closeness of the siege more than did that silence?) it was his voice, "which," says the *Globe*, "the English people had learned to trust for an authentic account of affairs at Khartoum," that once more made itself heard and on the 29th September last a telegram from him was published in the *Times*, which carried the story of the siege down to the 31st July

1884. Could, then, any further information from him, however slight, be without general interest?

I have said the letters are free from any literary pretensions. Written for his home circle only—some of them in illness, some of them piecemeal and at intervals between daily duties, some of them in hurried moments to catch an unexpected post—they are naturally careless in style. Then so thoughtful of those at home was he, so ever present were they in his mind, that in many of his letters allusions to home and to us all are so intermixed (by comparisons with things in our knowledge only or otherwise) with the descriptive matter that in omitting these the continuity of the letters is broken, and they appear much more disconnected than they really were in their entirety.

Except for such references to family and private matters, and occasionally some expressions of opinion which were so mingled with as to be inseparable from them, I have omitted nothing, and not in even the slightest degree altered the text of the letters.

No doubt, amid the strange surroundings and in the stirring times in which he lived, he might have written more fully than he did; but it should be borne in mind how he came to be in Khartoum at all, and his reasons for not doing so will be understood.

It was on May 17, 1883, that the late Edmond O'Donovan, the celebrated correspondent of the *Daily News,* whose name will be always associated with that of Merv, sailed from Gravesend in the Orient steamer *Cuzco, en route* for Khartoum there to attach himself to Hicks Pacha's army which, having beaten the Mahdi's lieutenants at Merebele, was resting there a breathing space before marching on the strongholds of the arch rebel himself in Khordofan. My brother accompanied Mr. O'Donovan. Their objects were similar, their purpose was partly a joint one Each was the correspondent of an English newspaper, and, as such, anxious to follow the fortunes of the campaign which Hicks Pacha was entering upon, and to chronicle its events. But, in addition, they had resolved to explore the country in the fullest manner, and to publish the result o their observations in a book. In inviting my brother to join him in this undertaking, Mr. O'Donovan had selected one who was not without qualifications for the task: ready with his pen, my brother had gained also some reputation with his pencil, and, though but twenty-five years of age when he set out for Khartoum, he had already done duty as a war correspondent on the Bulgarian frontier in the late Russo-Turkish War.

How within twelve days they crossed the desert route from Suakim to Berber, and, never delaying, pushed on thence to Khartoum—how they found Hicks Pacha's army there, and after a short interval accompanied its march towards Khordofan —all this is told in the letters which follow. O'Donovan fell in the fatal field of El Obeid, but my brother, saved by an illness which had made his life despaired of, found himself back once more in Khartoum, and, never relinquishing his original design, from thence kept note and account of everything that passed around him. Trusting that some day his book would see the light, he saw no reason to relate all his experiences and observations in his letters, but preferred rather to confine them to familiar descriptions of matters likely to interest those whom he loved at home. Hence, as I have said, his letters are less full and practical in detail than they might otherwise have been.

So much explanation of the circumstances in which they were written, so much apology for their shortcomings, seemed to me to be necessary; the interest which is contained in these letters, and their value, I leave to the reader's judgment to estimate.

ARNOLD POWER.

50 MERRION SQUARE, DUBLIN,
March 1885.

LETTERS FROM KHARTOUM.

Orient R.M. Steam Ship "Cuzco,"
off Plymouth,
May 18, 1883.

My dearest Mother,

Just a line by the shore-boat to say good-bye again. O'Donovan and myself are on board, *en route* to Ismailia, and I can only again write to you at Naples. We left Gravesend yesterday. We have the best state-room in the ship, which is an immense one; it brought out the Duke of Connaught and his staff to Egypt. I am very well, and the sea since we left has been like glass. The doctor on board is brother to E. D. Gray, M.P. I thought we should never leave London, we had so many things to buy: saddlery, photographic apparatus, and arms. O'Donovan presented me with the best rifle London could produce. We ran down to Liverpool on Saturday night, as O'Donovan wanted to see some friends. We dined with his brother, and came up again on Sunday night. Major Howett joined us to-day; he comes part of the way with us. The food on board is very good; and the saloon is like a conservatory with flowers.

You will of course remember me to all. Believe that I am indeed sorry to leave you on my present mission, but no doubt it is for the best. Fradelle will send the photograph. I send one of the ship. Tell A—— and M—— and all at home that I wish them every blessing, and I'm sure they do the same for me. It is almost impossible to write aboard ship. In any case my time is up. God bless you. Good-bye.

Yours——

FRANK POWER.

Write to H.M.'s Consul, Ismailia.

Hotel Royal, Cairo,
June 7, 1883.

Dearest Mother,

We had to run up here four days ago to get our firmans from the Khedive, and leave here for Suez in two days, and thence by Red Sea to Suakim. This is a delightful place, and full of English officers, but the heat is intense. One can only wear the thinnest Indian silk clothing and a white helmet.

This is an excellent hotel, and I found our old friend J. Rogers staying here—in fact, the hotel is like a barracks, and we are the only people not in uniform at meals.

Coming out in the *Cuzco* I met a **Mr. D——**, whose people have been very kind to me here; they gave a little dinner for us on Monday, where we met several distinguished men in command here. Next day we dined with Sir E. Malet, who got us our firmans, and on Wednesday, with the 35th, the guests of young Trevor (you know his people) and Powell, also a Dublin man. We lunched to-day with the 19th Hussars, and dined to-night with Rogers' fellows. To-morrow we ride to the Pyramids with C——, who commands the Egyptian new Cavalry; he is a very jolly fellow. General S—— comes with us. I enjoy the sight in the Schonraba Road in the evenings, when everybody turns out—the native ladies in carriages, &c.

I am looking forward to the big game in Kordofan, which I hear is the best in the world. We spent a day at Port Said, and a day and a night at Ismailia, which is the prettiest place I ever saw.

* * * * *

Good-bye.

FRANK POWER.

KHARTOUM, UPPER EGYPT,
August 2, 1883.

MY DEAREST MOTHER,

I arrived here last evening, after a fatiguing and unbroken journey of forty-three days. O'Donovan was ill in Cairo, and when he recovered we left Suez on an Egyptian Government steamer to go down the Red Sea. It was a small steamer, with 2,000 pilgrims on board—men, women, and children—bound for Mecca.

There was not an inch of any portion of the deck uncovered, and some had to stand by turns to let others lie down to rest. The steamer was a wretched one, the captain and crew Arabs. There was not one boat. I wonder we were not burned, as all the Hadjiis smoked and cooked their food wherever there was any room on deck. We got rid of them—Turcomans, Persians, Hindoos, Syrians, Cherkees, Bedawi, and Arabs—at Jedda, where we stayed three days, the guests of a Mr. O——, a wonderfully nice fellow.

Jedda is a walled and moated town; we used to almost fly to and from the ship (two miles over coral reefs) in dhows with enormous sails. We then went on to Suakim. The heat all the time was fearful; iron exposed to the sun burned you to the bone if you accidentally touched it. Hot drinking water, hot soles to your boots from the hot decks, hot animals to warm your bed in the bunk, and your very clothes too great a burden to bear, rendered the place intolerable; nor did the heat abate when we landed. Here the natives were in full dress, with a handkerchief, a bundle of charms on their elbow, a spear, sword, and shield for the males, and a dish-cloth and a silver nose-ring for the females. All wear sandals, but, like the Kerry country girls with their shoes, generally take them off when *walking*!

When we landed we heard the war drums beating, and in a large space between the tents (heaps of straw thrown on wattles) saw a fantasia with spear, shield, and sword. These people are very handsome, beautifully built, and like reddish-bronze statues. Their hair is very curious. They are the Haddandowahs tribe, descended, it is said, from the Queen of Sheba. I never saw one of them unarmed, but, though they look most fierce, are gentle, civil, good-natured fellows. Their tribe reaches to Berber. They are mountaineers. The next morning we got a guide and four camels —two with riding-saddles and two for baggage— filled our water-skins, and set off. First day, desert; fine sand and camel-thorn (mimosa). Second day, came to water-pool—water, you know, even in the Nile, is a rich, opaque, coffee-colour, but water in a desert-pool is not even liquid mud, and must be bailed in *blobs* (like custard) into the skins. Our little party of three passed hundreds of natives, Arab caravans, and Soudani negroes, ebony giants, a little liberal in the allowance of lips and feet; and, though all armed, hurting nobody. Then we got up amongst rocky, baking mountains, sandy passes, along river courses, here and there a flock of goats. I am a great hand at bagging, killing, and preparing a sheep or goat. For eight days rock and mountain, with occasional plateaux of sand and gravel, spotted with mimosa trees and bushes; here and there a gazelle (hard to hit). At one water-station, we found Ariab rock well, clear water, trees, shade, and sleep; other places seem too hot for sleep at midday halt. We used to go forward in the morning till 10.30, and then, from 2 in the afternoon till 8 o'clock, camp down; both halts make fire, and feed—tea, dates, ship-biscuits in hot water, and potted meats. In the day some ants (white, black, and red) and fifty other insects, down your shirt-collar and everywhere, like Macbeth, murdered sleep; at night we got some sleep. At first made large fires to keep off wild beasts, but then thought it better to sleep in the dark, as the light brought round us such very neighbourly desiring-to-make-your-acquaintance monsters—as scorpions and tarantulas. The bite of the scorpion is weeks of fever, and of the tarantula generally a funeral. We killed one of the latter four inches long in the body; his legs and all would just cover a small plate. I send you a drawing of a scorpion I got between my blouse and my vest; he is stuck by a pin on the top of my helmet. They come crawling over you, and will run at the smallest movement, and not touch you if left alone; but the danger is that when half asleep you feel one (generally on your face), you put up your hand and brush it off; then it lets fly at you.

Last two days, sand and desert, and then Berber and the Nile (over a mile wide). Berber is a hole of a place, but welcome after twelve days and nights on a camel-saddle (first day on camel merry h—ll). Got on wretched antiquated dirty tug-boat with two barges (soldiers' clothes, guns; eighty passengers sitting cross-legged on the cases), and off for Khartoum. (Of course the Arab lied when he said six days to Khartoum.) On this tug we were burnt into holes by sparks from its old wood-fire; overrun with cockroaches and "day-lighting rats," and an old scorpion come in with the firewood, so we might say we got them "fresh from the wood."

We "stubbed" up to the bank every evening, and slept on the mud or sand till morning. We also stopped for wood or whenever an Arab saw an acquaintance on the bank during the day; even then the thing would not stop snorting and throwing cascades of wood-sparks. The wily crocodile, in all lengths, from 1 foot to 30, seems to be the Conservancy Board of the river; and there are at least a thousand different sorts of storks and ibises. The niggers and Arabs are always jumping overboard for something or other —a bit of wood dropped or an old rag—to snatch a kid, a goat, or a fowl from the bank, and then swimming back and climbing in. I saw a fellow jump in after a piece of lemon I threw away just beside a crocodile, though that evening we had lost a man (cut in two) and heard of several being nipped at the villages. I suppose they get used to being killed. Here and there we bought some fowls, a kid, a lamb, or some eggs and dates. We got here after twenty-five days of the most wretched steamboat torture. The sunsets on the Nile, the river-side scenes, the palms, and the delightful quantity of mud in the water could not be rivalled.

After Berber the natives (ebony giants) wear a knife strapped to the elbow as their sole clothing; the women natives, a five-inch fringe of blue and white china beads strung on thread. General Hicks has given us a large room in the Government House, on the corridor of which the English, Irish, Austrian, and South African officers in the Egyptian service live. We each have a paved room with a divan at one end, and two large holes for windows which look out on the Nile. The gallery at the door runs round a yard with a well and some palm-trees with monkeys, and a convoy of £4,000 worth of elephants' tusks waiting to be sent down to Egypt; and, as each tusk has a lump of gum about the size of a leg of mutton stuck to it, the smell is fearful. The enemy, "the False Prophet," is in possession of the country ten miles from this city, and in about two weeks we begin the campaign. We await some rain, 6,000 men, and a battery. *A propos* of rain, one night on the way up we had a Niagara on our heads, and had, we might say, to dodge the forked lightning for hours. The Nile is now at its highest, and roars along at the rate of a railway train. We are just at the junction of the Blue and White Niles. We ascend the White one to Kawa and on to El Obeid. The heat here is fearful. My hands are so moist I can hardly keep this paper together. When writing, direct as above. I have not been frightened at your long silence, as I knew you did not know where to find us. In the desert and on the river I've always been thinking of you all at home, and hoping for a letter when I reached Khartoum. In this curious place, with its stately Arabs in their flowing white robes, and its niggers with their shining brown skins and deep black ones, it is queer to think of Merrion Square, but I often do so. I have just now heard a man with a tom-tom proclaiming that, if they get twenty letters, a post will start in an hour; therefore I hasten to get this off, though I could spin this yarn out for a week.

. . . . Excuse this hasty letter; I have not time to read it over.

* * * * *

FRANK POWER.

KHARTOUM,
September 1, 1883.

DEAREST ARNOLD,

* * * * *

I am well, notwithstanding the bad water and the confounded heat, and am now busy, as in three days we march on a campaign that even the most sanguine look forward to with the greatest gloom. We have here 9,000 infantry that fifty good men would rout in ten minutes; and 1,000 cavalry (Bashi-Bazouks) that have never learned even to ride, and these, with a few Nordenfeldt guns, are to beat the 69,000 men the Mahdi has got together. We go by the White Nile to El Douam (Duem), where a large hollow square will be formed, with 5,000 camels in the centre. In this form we will set out for El Obeid, about 250 miles.

That Egyptian officers and men are not worth the ammunition they throw away is well known, and the few black regiments we have will be left to garrison this place, as the Arabs and townspeople fear them. We will have a machine gun at each corner of the square.

The first stage is fifty miles to a desert well, which at best times cannot supply many, and here 12,000 men, close on 6,000 camels, and 3,000 horses, mules, and donkeys are to be watered; if, as the spies report, the well is poisoned or filled up by the Mahdi, we can never struggle back on our tracks, but must die there. Each well will, of course, be occupied by the Mahdi's men, and must be fought for. The Mahdi, within eighteen months, has won all along the line (except at Marabele, where Hicks beat his lieutenant), and during that time has taken prisoners or killed 16,000 Egyptian soldiers, taken 7,000 Remington rifles, 487,900 packets (of twelve each) of cartridges, eighteen guns, and one rocket battery. The spies report that the Arab officers he captured at El Obeid have become instructors; so, really, he has thousands of soldiers as well armed as ours, and he has gun practice daily. His 6,000 cavalry are banded together by oath, and if fifty of them get into our square, or one shell fall amongst our 5,000 camels, the whole thing is up. The people here believe that Mahomet Achmet is the real Mahdi foretold in the Koran, as he answers to the description, even to the mark on his nose; and even our own officers and men (a cowardly, beggarly mob) believe that he is a prophet, and are less than half-hearted in the business, so that the ruffianly though brave Bashi-Bazouks and the niggers are the only men to be relied on.

Every day, manifestoes from the Mahdi are stopped here. Three hundred miles away, on the desert route which we crossed from Suakim to Berber, 700 miles from the Mahdi's theatre of operations, his envoys have raised the natives, and 3,000 reinforcements and stores coming up from the Red Sea were beaten back and seized, so you see that 200 miles in our rear our communications are stopped; however, a dromedary-post goes by Assuan and Assiout, and by it this letter goes.

It is very dull here on the banks of the Blue Nile. We have a large room in the Staff House and a kitchen, and, as we have brought three slaves, are pretty comfortable. Our old cook is a Niam-Niam cannibal converted to Islamism, who has been to Mecca—she is a great character. The slave trade is in full swing here again, there being over 27,000 registered slaves here; they are very well treated, and are always happy, and I would like them only for their infernal tom-toming all night under the palms outside. They seem to sing and dance all night, and are representatives of all the races of Central Africa. We have here on the staff of General Hicks, who is a wonderfully good fellow, Colonel Farquhar, Colonel de Coëtlogan, Major Evans, interpreter, Baron de Sheckendorff, Major von Herlt, Major Massey, Major Warner, Captain Matyuga. Martin Walker and Colborne are invalided back to Cairo. We nearly all live together, but my chum, Von Herlt, has gone over the river to take command of the cavalry. We have our tent, food for three months (we can only march seven miles a day), camels, &c., and two dromedaries, or quick camels, for riding, ready. All letters sent to Khartoum will come on. Every night when we halt there will be a zereba, or thick rampart of thorns, put round the square, and, outside this, wires stretched to trip the natives, and the whole ground strewn with crows' feet (caltorps) —eight iron spikes in a cluster—to tickle the bare feet of the Kordofani. I believe their rush is wonderful; they had only their spears and shields in the other battles, and, in spite of the Nordenfeldts, Remingtons, &c., they swept over the square. At Mirabele they reached within six yards of the square, in the face of 7,000 breech-loaders and the artillery.

I am not ashamed to say I feel the greatest sympathy for them, and every race that fights against the rule of Pachas, backsheesh, bribery, robbery, and corruption. I pity Hicks; he is an able, good, and energetic man, but he has to do with wretched Egyptians, who take a pleasure in being incompetent, thwarting one, delaying, and lying. We heard here to-day that James Carey had been shot, and the Duke of Marlborough is dead; so you see we are not out of the world. An old newspaper here is worth a pound. I think, if one had something to read, it would take his mind off this Nile water-rash, with which we are all covered, and which occupies one's undivided attention to scratch. I don't think I sleep one night in ten from it. I am very thin, but in excellent health (barring the rash), which here is a sign of rude health, and have a black beard, which I wear *à la* Vandyke; my hair cut as short as possible. I wear a pair of long boots, riding-breeches, a white tunic and necktie, a solar helmet, with a crimson silk puggaree, and a crimson cummerbund under my belt. If you leave off this latter you would be at once down with dysentery. We are very natty and tidy here, and the fellows turn out as neat as if they were going to an "at-home." There is an Austrian Mission here, and it is so queer to hear the chapel-bell ringing the Angelus each day among the palm-trees, and above the clatter of Arabs, slaves, naked men and women, and the cries of tropical birds. We hope to rescue some of the priests and two nuns who are with the Mahdi, but the belief is they are killed. The Mission garden is a Paradise, and their chapel a little gem. Their schools are attended by slaves, and they do a great deal of good here. The rest of the European colony consist of Greek merchants, a d——d lot of Jews who would rob their grandmothers. Excuse mistakes in this letter, as outside the window soldiers are loading the barges with food, &c., and, along with the water-carriers, women washing, Arab boys fighting, are making an infernal din, and Sheckendorff has his feet upon the table singing a German version of La-di-da. I can't tell how anxious I am to hear about all at home. . . . .

* * * * *

Yours,

FRANK POWER.

KHARTOUM,
October 9, 1883.

DEAREST MOTHER,

It would be impossible to describe my feelings on getting home-letters yesterday, particularly as I had just been on the point of never hearing from any of you in this world again. Your and ——'s letters I'm sure have done me more good than all the medicine the Arab doctor,

Fadlaheen bey Effendi, can give me, and I now feel better. . . . .

However, first I must tell you how I come to be back here. After a month's stay in Khartoum, where I made hosts of friends, we, with all the staff, crossed the White Nile to Onderman, to commence our long march to El Obeid, the capital of the Kordofan (you will find both marked on the atlas). The next morning we set out with 5,000 to 6,000 camels (a nice lot to bring through a hostile country), 9,000 men, 1,000 cavalry, 2 Krupp batteries, Nordenfeldts, and 20 light guns. I travelled on a splendid dromedary given me by Aladeen Pacha, the Governor-General, but, either from heat or the water-skins, &c., on the third day I was down with dysentery. The doctor with the staff knew nothing, and I got weaker and weaker, and next day had to be led on a horse with two soldiers to hold me on. There was no ambulance, and the Mahdi's cavalry were hovering behind, so no person could be left even to rest. It wasn't pleasant for a person who could not walk to have to sit up under 127 degrees of heat, no shade, and a knowledge that every drop of water one drunk made him worse. On the fifth day I had to be put on one of the Krupp cannons, which eight horses drew over rocks, stones, trunks of trees, &c., so it was no easy mode of travelling. At last we got to Duaime (Duem), a port on the Nile, after a 250-mile march. On the arrival of Georges Bey, Surgeon-General to the Soudan, he at once told the General to send me back to Khartoum, as I was utterly unfit for another day's march, so four soldiers carried me down to the *Bourdain*, the Governor-General's steamer, and in two days I was back in Khartoum, where an Arab doctor (an excellent one) nearly cured me, along with the great care and nursing Colonel de Coëtlogan gave me. He is in command here, and is the only Englishman here now; he has lodged me in the Palace. He had to go in the steamer to patrol the White Nile. He did not like to leave me alone, and, as the doctor said the change of air would do me good, he took me with him. We left this day week. I had everything I wanted, but the first day out I got a relapse, and up to yesterday was very bad. We have just come back here, but I cannot yet walk, and write this lying down on my angerib or wicker-bed. I was very low-spirited at being invalided back, and so losing all chance of fighting, but De Coëtlogan is such a good fellow and has been so kind to me he has quite cheered me up. Now that I am stronger I've sent a column and a-half to the *Times*, and, if I am able, to-morrow will send another letter to them, and I've sent off a lot of sketches to the *Pictorial*. . . . . I get on very well with the Arabs, and must try and perfect myself in Arabic. You would scarcely know me. I now weigh 9 stone; three months ago I was 14 stone 5. I have taken off my beard, and my face is laughably thin. We (De Coëtlogan and self) went in the steamer away to the Shilloke savage country beyond Kordofan and back here. We had 100 soldiers and two guns with us, and captured five of the Mahdi's boats after a smart fire. I am very sorry not to be up with the column, as to-day or to-morrow there will be a great battle, but we can get no man to venture on a dromedary with the post to the army, as the last was caught and put into an ant-hill alive. Tell Arnold to look up a file of the *Times* a week or two before you get this, as there is more news in it, for, though

I am only writing for ten minutes at a time, I am not strong enough to go on much longer. Send me as many papers as you can, as I must lie on my back all day watching the flies, and have nothing to read. I saw about Lord L—— in a *Vanity Fair* the General lent me in camp.

* * * * *

The climate of Khartoum is lovely, always shade from the palm and lemon trees. I told you before about the Austrian Mission, where there is Mass every morning ; I hear the bells ringing now for the office for Pater Franciscus, who died (I hear) yesterday. The Mahdi put a lot of them to death at El Obeid. The Archbishop of Central Africa lives here, and there is a convent of Sisters of Mercy, who are greatly beloved by the Arabs. I fear you will think this letter very egotistical, but I know you take an interest in all that concerns me. I was glad to get M——'s budget of home news. Remember me to Mr. and Mrs. M——. I was so sorry he was beaten in his election by a Land Leaguer. Excuse this straggling letter ; but, as my soldier servant, who sits up with me at night, says :

"Ham-d-il-illah fi bocqra quies." (With God's mercy, I will be better to-morrow.)

* * * * *

FRANK POWER.

P.S.—Friday, *October* 11, 1883.—As the post does not go until to-day, I have kept back my scrawl until the last. I am much better, and am getting stronger day by day, and hope to be able to leave with Colonel de Coëtlogan on Sunday for another trip on the river. To-day is the first day of the great Mussulman feast, the Bairam, and the troops are marching past to a review, and cannons are banging in all directions. As the Pachas and Beys went past with their staffs they all pulled up to say "Salaam," and to hope I was better, and each sent a slave the first thing in the morning with a bouquet of flowers, and to hope, as it was a feast, that Allah would make me well. I have not for six days, until to-day, taken anything but milk and lemon with sugar and water. To-day De Coëtlogan sent me down a tin of Crosse and Blackwell's oatmeal, and I had a splendid dish of stirabout and milk. Old Hadjia (the cook) tells me she used to make it for Sir Samuel and Lady Baker every morning when they were travelling through Africa." Ijia and the soldier are going off to the feast. I gave her a string of yellow glass beads for her bald head; she says she is only sixty-five, but hopes the beads will get her a husband (she is a widow since 1850). The row outside is fearful; the niggers all tom-toming and banjoing like mad, with new pieces of linen round them (their only clothing). Though they are all slaves and pagans, they really seem to enter into all the Mussulman festivals as if they were made for them. Hadjia is a Niam-Niam cannibal; but has been for fifty years, since Petterick freed her, a Mussulman, and at her own expense took the pilgrimage to Mecca, and then went to see Constantinople. She has made a lot of money (she was cook to Gordon and Baker Pachas), and she lets it out at 50 per cent. to other blacks; and she has six slaves for hire at three dollars a month; yet she cooks, washes, &c., for me at two dollars, and if she gets an old bottle or meat tin she is off to sell it for a farthing.

She gets me things very cheaply, as the people

in the bazaar are afraid of her tongue. She slanged Ibraham Pacha this morning for calling out at the window while I was asleep; she is quite a character, and smokes a short red clay pipe all day, and says her prayers every ten minutes. There is a post here to-day; I am eagerly looking forward to letters. . . . .

7 o'clock P.M.

The chief of the Austrian Mission has just sent me 100 fresh limes from their garden for lemonade, which is most acceptable. Thousands of natives are crossing the Blue Nile, under my windows, to a great fantasia or *fête* in the village on the other side. The little boats with their enormous white sails are laden almost to sinking. Hadjia, who has turned up with an enormous drum and a sleeping mat, has got the halfpenny for the ferry money from me, and is gone over to howl and dance till 4 o'clock in the morning; she has about half a pound of tobacco in an old rag and a box of matches, and says 'tis the happiest day in her life. She has seven grandchildren with her, all as black as jet, and each for its entire dress a string of beads on its neck and a ring in the side of its lip or nose. Until kids are twelve or thirteen here, they go without any clothing whatever.

* * * * *

FRANK POWER.

KHARTOUM,
October 27, 1883.

DEAREST MARY,

As in my last letter to mother I told her of my illness, I know both you and she will be anxious to hear how I am. After forty days' severe illness, I am now getting on like "a house on fire." I'm as strong as ever on the pins, and walk a great deal, as the weather has, owing to the commencement of the north winds, become delightfully cool, yet the middle hours of the day, from 5 o'clock to 10 o'clock (in European time from 11 A.M. to 4 P.M.), are too hot for a person to venture out. A cool wind is always blowing from the Nile now, and the boats, with their numerous white wing-like sails, are scudding up from the north. As I write I have a weight on the paper to keep it from blowing away (a thing you will hardly believe of Africa), and also to keep the enormous black ants that infest this house from dragging it away! (this is an exaggeration). I am alone here. Colonel de Coëtlogan is on the White Nile with his steamer; he goes away every Sunday and returns every Saturday. I was not well enough to go with him the last two trips, and, as there is now no one here who speaks English, it is so much the better for my Arabic, which I already speak as well as I do German. It might enable me to get a Consulship hereafter. I think on Sunday De Coëtlogan will go up the Blue Nile to Sennaar as far as the Abyssinian frontier; if so, I will go for the change. It is now thirty-two days since Hicks Pacha and his immense army marched from Duem, where I left, and since then *not one word, good or bad*, has been heard of him or his 11,000 men. The "word of mouth" among the tribes travels quick as telegraph, yet no news. When it comes it must be good, as no such army has ever been seen before in those parts. If it is bad, we,

Christians, Turks, and Cairo Arabs here, will not have ten minutes to live, as the Arabs here are to a man secretly for the Mahdi. Passing my windows they called out to me, " Have you heard from your General yet ? "—under the very nose of my guard-room, for at my gate I am master of the bodies and souls of a sergeant and twenty-five six-foot nigger regulars, who " turn out " if I go in or out.

I am up at 4 o'clock (franghi time) every morning, have my cup of tea, and go to sit in the big place or square until 10 o'clock under the great palm-tree of Polycratus. At the *café* I meet the Pachas and Beys and see about 1,000 Arabs, niggers, slaves, and others doing their marketing along the stalls and booths of the bazaar. It is a picture no description or sketch could give you an idea of, from the Arab of the desert on his dromedary to the serpent-charmer, or from the dervish or to the passing Pacha on his ass, every one bargaining over fruit, fish, flesh, and firewood, and above all the voices you can catch Hadjia's; she is a great *connaisseuse* of sheep or cow slaughtering, and must see four or five killed before she sees a joint to her liking, and she is splendid at knocking a farthing off a quartern loaf, or its equivalent here. I do my sketches and write to the *Times* during the hours which the sun keeps me indoors, and pray that I may soon get other papers from home. I got your *Mail* last Sunday, and now know it by heart. I thought I was once again speaking to Dr. Shaw, F.T.C.D., when I read the leader. This is the Arab Sabbath, and the niggers, with their tom-toms, on the ships outside are hard at work, so I'm "well-nigh moidered" while I write, but generally it is very quiet and solitary here. The river, the desert beyond, the palm-trees, and everything, even to the ships and costumes (unchanged since the waves were stilled on Galilee), serve to remind one that there is a good God, but the ignorance, the mind-darkness, and the wretchedness of the people sometimes make one think that God has forgotten or turned His back on this land of misfortune, but, on reflection, when one sees all that is good here, it only makes him think how great and inscrutable His ways are, and one (if one has a heart) must remember that in justice God will save all these poor people, who never had a chance of knowing Him, and who live as well as Nature teaches them, and, as Mussulmen, never transgress the laws of the only religion God has permitted them to know. If the Irish tenant were here, would he take twenty years more of life and exchange with him? If they wish to grow corn they must pay for permission to do so, pay for liberty to take water from the broad Nile (without which the land is a sand desert), and pay for liberty to sell the corn. If the crop is good, pay double taxes (one for the private purse of the Pacha and one for the Government at Cairo). If they don't grow the corn they can't pay the taxes at all, and are kourbashed (good hippopotamus hide) and put into prison. No matter how they make a few piastres, the dragoman of some Bey or Pacha will steal it for his master. They frequently pull down huts and tear up yards and fields to find where the coins are hidden. If the peasant buys a few rags for his wife or child, or mends a hole in his hut to keep out the sun, he is told he must have got money somewhere, and he is doubly taxed, and after all his sole possessions are a hut made of mud and river reeds, a rush angerib or bed, a rush mat, and an earthen pot. If God gives him this poverty-stricken life, one remembers that He has also taught him to consider raw or boiled corn, now and then a bit of fish or meat and some water, food for a king, and never to desire any more, for envy and ambition are unknown here. I wish some of the Irish agitators had a year of it. If you were in the bazaars here you would see a thousand and one things you would like to set off your house with (not to be got at home, but of no value here), but the distance forbids their transmission.

Talking of buying, I have just spent four dollars and bought out and liberated a very handsome little slave servant who was fearfully beaten by his master, and the little wretch has come and asked me to let him be a slave again, as then he would have no anxiety as to how he could get his food. As, by law, he is mine, I have taken him on, and given him an old flannel shirt and a fez. When he came to me he was stark naked, with two verses of the Koran rolled in raw hide tied to his ankles to prevent him in the dark from falling into a pit or well. He has, like all his tribe, more intelligence than a young Newton. As a Dinka savage, he believed in an unknown God, who would one day come to regenerate the world; as a Mussulman slave, he was told to believe in Allah, but he says the Turkish Allah only gave him a raw back and the kourbash every morning, and an earthen floor to sleep on; he was told to believe that our God was Aba-el-Kanzir, the father of all pigs.

He is eight years old, and I have spent four hours in my limited Arabic trying to explain to him about our God and what He had done for us, but it would have puzzled a theologian to answer the questions this brat put to me, but I hope to have him baptized before very long, and, as he is able to shave me every morning, help Hadjia, who calls him the "father of all dogs," and even beat her at a bargain in the bazaar, I will keep him. He thinks, if he becomes a Christian, and goes with me to England, he will become white and have a moustache. As, before I had him two hours he had called Michaelovich Bey, the Albanian Colonel of Police, a fool because he wore a beard, stood on his head in the balcony while I was bowing at the window to the Pacha, and slanged every nigger sailor on the ships outside, I have christened him the "*enfant terrible.*" He has just eaten my last pot of Crosse and Blackwell's greengage jam, but when I get him into shape he will be a treasure, as he is very much attached to me. He has no relative in the world. The brains and intelligence of these poor savages are wonderful; yet though made to be a leading race, they have no hope beyond being slaves, eating four pounds of elephant or hippopotamus flesh at a sitting, and some day " entering the crocodile's stomach "—so they call dying. . . . . You must be sick of Soudani politics now, so I will drop it. To show you the dulness here, I send you a few days torn from my diary, little to enter and no secrets to let out. The "*enfant terrible*" proposes new excitements every ten minutes, such as " If the Hadjia will take a felac [small boat], at two groschen, and come to the Sand Island at Undurman, I will show him where an old crocodile is watching her eggs. Her tail will be good roasted with locusts;" or " Effendi, outside the city at the stork's tree there is a great serpent; I'll carry the axe, and serpents' glurba [soup] is splendid" (gniesse); but the E. T.—whose name, by-the-way, is Islamann—is disregarded, and I am lowered in the estimation of this slave, whose only garment when on his feet is a red shirt, but who by standing on his head ten-minutely returns to his original full-dress nakedness. I am often mean enough to remind him that he cost me the price of a small loaf of sugar, and it is whiter than he is, but he winks and puts in his "Mafi min sukerich" (but not so sweet). These things pass my day. It is night while I write this, and the dogs, frogs, and donkey are bursting their lungs to make a Handel Festival outside, and the crickets in the room chime in as a triangle at the end of each bar. A Greek gentleman (the worse of the bottle) has just come in, but, as they are mostly robbers, I gave him a cigarette and wished Kaleo Noctie, as he says, and told the sergeant to show him out—the worst of having a light on your balcony.

Saturday.—There is no more news to tell. Excuse my writing; my letter last night was finished by the light of the moon and the wind blowing the paper about. I hope to have some letters to-morrow.

* * * * *

FRANK POWER.

KHARTOUM,
November 3, 1883.

MY DEAREST ARNOLD,

* * * * *

I am still very weak; this dysentery has stuck to me for fifty days—a spell long enough to kill most men, but I feel right enough, only that to button my collar or tie my tie fatigues me. Writing is a martyrdom to me, but it is like speaking to some one at home, and I have a "cacoethes scribendi" on me. It has, outside the hot hours, become really cold here, and a bitter wind howls all night. I revel in it, but the Egyptians wear furs. *A propos* of furs, you can get a fresh leopard or lion skin here for about two shillings, and ostrich feathers for a song. The dusting brushes in the shops are nearly all made of ostrich feathers. They are brought in by the hunters fresh; the reason they are so dear in Europe is, they will not stand the journey. We also have lions, rhinoceri, and giraffes here. . . . .

I hope to get letters soon. Two posts a week come on here, Sunday and Thursday, but only one goes out, on Saturday. I telegraphed to London Arab reports of the great battles gained by Hicks. Still not one word from the army itself or General. . . . .

FRANK POWER.

Gibelain, White Nile,
Tuesday, November 13, 1883.

My dearest Arnold,

I got your more than kind letter along with one from mother and some papers from M—— M—— just as we were leaving Khartoum on Sunday week for a short patrol on the White Nile. I really cannot tell you how glad I was to get the letters, and yours, dear Arnold, shows your usual great good nature. I had just written and posted my letter to you before I got yours. Colonel de

Coëtlogan is continually patrolling the White Nile, but he comes back to Khartoum every Saturday. This time I was strong enough to go with him. Since the General left Duem on the 25th of September not one word has been heard—only the reports that Arabs bring in; he is supposed to have beaten the Mahdi in seven battles and to be at El Obeid, but his provisions must be almost out, and it is certain death for any one who tries to carry a letter to or from him. There is the greatest anxiety felt in Khartoum, and they telegraph twice a day from Cairo to know if we have tidings, but no one can say for certain. The news must come first to Duem, between here and Khartoum, and Colonel de Coëtlogan goes there every second day in his fast steamer the *Bourdain*, so desirous is he to know about the army. We sleep on the quarter-deck every night in our angeribs. It is delightfully cool; in fact, all day a cool breeze blows now, and it is downright cold at night. We are 350 miles nearer the Equator than Khartoum. It is very wild on both banks, and full of game. There are an old lion and lioness that roar all night at the water's edge, but the jungle is so thick that one could not get a shot from the steamer. We are daily cutting off the retreat of fugitive rebels, and have now seized all the boats on the river except the Shillook canoes, as they are friendly. We got the last boat the day before yesterday; she was sunk next the bank to hide her, and there were Arabs on guard. We threw two four-inch shells and gave them a volley, and they fired back and ran : on landing the long boat, we captured about 1,000 dollars' worth of stuff and some shields and spears, and we are now running down to Duem.

Duem, White Nile.

No news whatever of Hicks here yet, though this is his base of operations, and is full of stores, thousands of tons of biscuits, &c., but nothing can go outside the town, which is surrounded by a trench and rampart. There are about 1,500 rebel cavalry, which come within half a mile of the town every day; and, yesterday, a camel man and his three camels were snatched up almost at the gate. On our arriving last night, we heard five Remington shots, and Colonel de Coëtlogan got his men ready, and ran the steamer to the north end of the rampart to enfilade with his gun the rebels; but we could see nothing. It was only some sentries who noticed horsemen out on the plain, and fired. The rebels fell back. The Governor here, Said Bey, a nigger, is a frightful beast, I believe in the pay of the Mahdi. He does nothing he is told, and takes no precautions. We will be back in Khartoum on Thursday. I telegraph every week to London. The wires run right to Khartoum, and (until the rebels cut them) on to here, El Obeid, and the Equator. I have never heard from the *Pictorial World*. Several of my sketches I believe to have been stolen each time the Berber rebels sacked the mails. I hope you will get this letter on your birthday. I have many a little curiosity I would like to send you, but no way to send it. However, I wish you from the bottom of my heart many, many happy returns. I must finish, as the boat is leaving. Colonel de Coëtlogan desires me to say that if it wasn't for him I shouldn't be alive (this *he* means as a joke, but it is nevertheless quite true).

* * * * *

FRANK POWER.

KHARTOUM,
November 24, 1883.

DEAREST ARNOLD,

Just a line to wish you all the usual Merry Christmas. I would write a long letter (it would arrive on Christmas Day) were I not almost sure that the Government **will** intercept this letter, as they have done all telegrams these last few days. Hicks, his staff, O'Donovan, and 12,000 men have been massacred. Colonel de Coëtlogan and I are in Khartoum, where, for the moment, the volcano has not **yet** " erupted ;" but the Mahdi has 300,000 men, with rifles and artillery, and we **have** only 2,000 soldiers, no retreat, and the town and the country to the Red Sea red hot for the rebels. However, **I'm in** excellent spirits, and as yet see little or no danger. I hope you will have many happy Christmases. If **I** am here, I will make Hadjia roast **me** some beef, buy me a turkey, and I'll pick up a tin **of** potted ham ; this, with a bottle of lager beer and the sun something dreadful in the shade, dressed in white linen and a solar topee, will make it quite Christmas. I write to you because I would only write a long Christmas letter to mother, and I've no wish for the interpreter of the Pacha, when he prigs this letter, to have a laugh over it. I know that Christmas is never anything but a mockery, except to those who earn at least one good dinner in the year by writing Christmas stories for the serials, and those who sell Christmas cards, or send in their quarterly bills. I am now living in the Palace here, in poor Hicks' suite of rooms. They are as he walked out of them; his gloves, papers, guns, &c., lying about; and one almost expects his ghost to come in, like the Commendatore in "Don Juan." You see this dysentery that I cursed and swore at so much saved my life, and "once out of the fire always out of the fire." If my first wire to the *Times* about poor Hicks got through in time I am all right. It is a study to see the different degrees of dignified funk shown by the Egyptian officers here, and each fellow's desire to be away out of the place. Imagine de Coëtlogan and I watching their retreating forms, a sort of Consul Mario (he was a tenor!) sitting on the ruins of a cartridge case, scaring the servants of the Mahdi with a look; you see I make a historical allusion, but it got mixed some way! . . . .

Next Christmas I hope to spend with you all, but I'll have to borrow a sealskin cloak from one of the girls, I shall feel the cold so much. . . . . I've no news to tell; my telegram to the *Times* told all the sad news of the pass at Kashgate. I feel deeply sorry for all, especially poor Arthur Herlt, who commanded Hicks' cavalry; he and O'Donovan are those I regret most. As each Egyptian soldier has at least two wives and a mud-hovel full of children, about 25,000 fellaheen widows and 300,000 poor brown children are penniless in Lower Egypt!

* * * * *

FRANK POWER.

KHARTOUM,
December 1, 1883.

MY DEAREST MOTHER,

I write you just a line to wish you many happy New Years, and to say that I am quite well and most cheerful. You see my *Times* telegrams, and I wrote to Arnold last week. I am of course very sorry for all the poor fellows slaughtered in Kordofan, and think what a narrow squeak I had. Was it not Providence sent me that severe illness? Only for it my bones would be fit for a museum, they would be so well picked. Mons. Marquet, the millionaire merchant here and French Consul, leaves to-day; he gave a great farewell dinner last night. Imagine in the Soudan a *salon* superior to many in Paris—wax-lights, mirrors, ten servants in livery, cut-glass, silver, and flowers; a dinner thoroughly Parisian turned out by his French *chef*; champagne, hock, claret, &c. We were ten —Colonel de Coëtlogan, the Governor-General, Commander-in-Chief, &c. Marquet's garden costs him a fortune; so we had green-peas, mushrooms, asparagus, &c., and every fruit, from strawberries to pineapples. Colonel de Coëtlogan and I mess together now; old Hadjia cooks for both, and the Colonel is delighted with her. I have taken over the mess presidency, as I speak Arabic. I sat next Ibraham Pacha last night, and was able to keep up the conversation all night without an interpreter, and got many compliments on my quickness in learning the language. I can now understand all they say, and ask for everything I want in Arabic.

I sincerely hope you have got over the winter without bronchitis; if you wintered here you would not fear it, but, though it is very hot, we don't feel it so much in here, as we have large airy rooms, with long colonnades and verandas, and are the only two living in the Palace. Gordon, Sir Samuel Baker, Hicks, &c., occupied my room at different times. I generally sleep on Colonel de Coëtlogan's divan, and we chat all night. We mess in the corridor, and have an Indian punkah over the table. We have sentries everywhere, and as many men-servants (soldiers) as we want. I have disturbed nothing of poor Hicks', and his photos, guns, and papers, &c., are lying about as if he only went out for a few moments. As long as I think you are all right at home I have no questions to ask, so my letters must appear egotistical. I am getting stronger every day, always walking or riding. . . . . We will be able to hold out here for months, and will be comfortable enough if the townspeople don't rise and if the reinforcements hurry up, but these latter will have to fight through 250 miles of mountains and defiles from **Suakim** to Berber; and even Baker Pacha (Valentine, not Sir Samuel, worse luck) may get "Hicksed" on the road. The exodus here is going on. Greeks, Copts, Turks, Maltese, Bengalese, Madrasees, Algerians, Italians—consuls and merchants—and οἱ πολλοι; all trooping down before the river to Berber is closed. Anyway, until Baker's army clears the Suakim route, they must stop at Berber, or cross the Nubian desert to Assuan eight days and eight nights without stopping, through a waste of sand, and every drop of water to be carried from the start; this is how the post is carried—a sort of camel-pony post.

*　　*　　*　　*　　*

FRANK POWER.

KHARTOUM,
December 6, 1883.

MY DEAREST ANGELA,

    *   *   *   *   *

I got papers from Mary to-day. Colonel de Coëtlogan and I are the last of the "Mulligans." All the Consuls and Europeans have left. I've got a telegram to-night that Sennaar "is riz" and gone for the Mahdi. The country is all up, and food is at famine prices, but old Hadjia still drives her bargains at the bazaar. . . . . The Palace is fearfully big and lonely. We hope Baker Pacha and his army will be here in six weeks to our relief. We have only 2,000 men to man four miles of earthworks and keep a rebel population of 60,000 Arabs quiet. I am kept busy. I constantly get telegrams from *Times* (relatives asking about staff officers). I answer them, and send my correspondence, so I've plenty to do.

    *   *   *   *   *

This letter is very short, but I quite forgot it was so near post-hour.

Your loving brother,
FRANK POWER.

KHARTOUM,
December 14, 1883.

MY DEAREST MOTHER,

I was rather put out to-day on seeing a Cairo paper which said I was wounded, a prisoner of the Mahdi, and the only European survivor of the massacre of Kashgate. My first thought was that this would be in the English papers, and that you might see it, and I was going to wire to you, but then I remembered my telegram to the *Times*, saying I was well and in Khartoum, must have reached your eye as soon as the false report. I was sorry to hear of poor E——'s accident, and glad to hear that J—— had got a good ship. To-day I got an unexpected telegram from Sir Evelyn Baring asking me to act as British Consul here; of course I accepted at once, as this does not prevent me from acting as *Times* correspondent. There were a few Hindoos, Cyprians, and Maltese, but they have all fled, having made a great outcry about their being British subjects, and having no Consul, and being forced to put themselves under the protection of the Persian Consul. I heard to-day that Captain Moncrieff, that I met in Djeddah, and who was Consul at Suakim, was killed near that place by the rebels. I was surprised at getting the consulship, but I suppose Sir E. Baring saw that in a crisis like the present he should have a Consul here, and, no possibility of one arriving from outside, and knowing I was here, has asked me to act. The Hindoo merchants have a lot of merchandise stored here. There is an English prisoner with the Mahdi, and the friends of the dead officers may require their traps to be sealed up and sent home. Arabs coming in every day confirm the news of the massacre.

The last that was seen of poor old Hicks was his taking his revolver in one hand and his sword in the other; calling on his soldiers to fix bayonets, and his staff to follow him, he spurred at the head of his troops into the dense mass of naked Arabs, and perished with all his men. They had fought for three days and nights without a drop of water, the whole day under a scorching sun on a sandy plain. The Arabs say the Mahdi lost 50,000 men in the three days, but they have no idea of figures. However, Hicks had 12,000 men, each with 200 cartridges, 36 cannon, and plenty of shells, and it was not till the last cartouche and shell were fired that the massacre took place. . . . . I read the Irish papers with great interest; they make life less monotonous here; but Baker Pacha and his army, with plenty of European officers, will be here in a few weeks, and we will have some stir; we are looking out anxiously for it. I am glad to see the Orangemen are meeting the Land League on its own ground; but they are foolish to resuscitate their obsolete old war-cries too much, as they will repel the respectable Catholics, who, being honest, do not believe that " Parnell is Allah, and Healy is his prophet." Of course the Mansion House balls are tabooed this year as well as last. . . . . I commenced this letter last night, and finish it now, 6 o'clock in the morning. Would you believe it is bitterly cold? I've warm clothes and a muffler on me; but before an hour I will find the heat excessive at breakfast, and we must have the punkah going to give us a breeze. It is a queer climate. There was one shower of rain here, I'm told, during the last two years (last August). Now that the sun is beginning to get hot, the Nile looks lovely. There is a crowd of snow-white-sailed ships starting for Sennaar; not a ripple on the water; the village opposite, the fringe of palm-trees, a field of durra, and the red desert away into the distance beyond: all a lovely picture. I am writing in the veranda, and overhead are enormous clusters of rich purple grapes and fresh green leaves hanging from the trellis. Here fruit comes in twice a year; there are grapes also ripe in June, and they are quite like hot-house fruits, and very cheap. I often think of you all at home, and imagine what you are doing at such and such an hour. There is an hour and twenty-five minutes difference in the time. . . . .

FRANK POWER.

KHARTOUM,
December 22, 1883.

DEAREST FANNIE,

As this is the **last post before** Christmas, I write to renew my good **wishes**. I yesterday got a telegram permitting **me to keep on the** *Times* and the Consulship at the same time. Thank mother very much for the letters enclosed. They may be of the greatest use to me as credentials if I return to Lower Egypt, but the Shakespeare has not arrived yet. Some haughty Bedawi is studying the works of the " Swan of Avon." That and the " Professor " and "Autocrat at the Breakfast Table" are the most welcome books I could have sent me. We have hit upon a few old copies of Dumas' works, and they gave us some reading for a time. I've bought a whopping turkey for dinner on Christmas Day. He is an enormous fellow, and gobbles all over the place. . . . . We (this is our most important topic here) are anxiously awaiting the relieving troops. We hope to see them here in about fifteen days, and then " Monsieur le Mahdi " may come on when he likes. The Mission has left, so I cannot go to church on Christmas Day. This letter must be full of mistakes, and very unconnected, as there are two Pachas and five others in the room holding a council of war very much at the top of their voices.

*   *   *   *   *

FRANK POWER.

KHARTOUM,
December 26, 1883.

DEAREST MOTHER,

We are all right, and I'm very happy. Yesterday was not such a bad Christmas Day after all. . . . . The two Pachas, hearing it was our "Bairam," or feast, called, first one and then the other, with their staff; we gave them coffee, curaçoa, and cigarettes. At dinner came my masterpiece (I'm housekeeper) the mammoth turkey, so we kept up the eating part of the festival, at least, you will perceive. We had our new cook yesterday; she is a great success. I think she is a Dinka native, but she wears clothes (a dress of the mode in fashion about the time Millais illustrated Trollope's books—long in the waist, flounces, and crinoline). She also revels in silver bangles on her arms, and one in the side of her lower lip, and a magnificent red silk handkerchief. I manage the house, as it gives me something to do; I hope I'll have no more trouble with servants. I had to sack old Hadjia; she never had dinner within two hours of the right time, and sometimes, without any notice, would be absent for the whole day.

Islamann, the boy, is getting on very well. Life is so quiet you will excuse me if I make use of domestic matters to fill my sheets. We heard yesterday from one of our spies that the Mahdi has commenced his march towards Sennaar and Khartoum; if he comes before our reinforcements dawdle up from Cairo, he can easily walk through the place. The works protecting the town are nearly four miles long, and we have not 2,000 soldiers to man them, and this would not permit us to have a patrol or a policeman in a city in which there are 15,000 avowed rebels, all with arms in their houses. The reinforcements should have been here long ago, but those wretched officials, &c., at Cairo move slowly when there is not a prospect of backsheesh about. However, the first relieving column should be here in twelve days. I wire nearly every day to Sir E. Baring and to the *Times*. As I write, a steamer and thirty barges, carrying the garrisons of Fashoda, down near Lake Albert Nyanza, 600 miles away, arrived. There are 2,000 old soldiers on them. This is most opportune, as to-morrow the festival Moorab-el-Nabi (the birthday of the Prophet) comes on.

The Arabs have set up a pole sixty feet high in the market-place, and will assemble round it in thousands to-morrow and for five days. This is bad, as the feast calls forth great religious excitement, and there are 15,000 here against the Government. There are thirty men in high positions here known to be their leaders, and we are not strong enough to seize them and openly hang them. The other night the Governor made the cool proposition to poison them. Colonel de Coëtlogan would not listen to this. He then said their servants were in his pay, and they could be secretly strangled in bed. This did not go down either, so we are content to wait, and hope they will keep quiet until the relief from Cairo arrive. To-night has doubled our garrison here, and in a few days the garrisons of Koneh and Duem will arrive (4,000 men).

I have spent the whole day arranging a magnificent trophy of spears, swords, arrows, war-horns, daggers, leopard and lion skins, native pipes, &c., on my wall. You know that I always went in for that kind of thing. I hope I shall be able to get my collection to England. I have a pistol that belonged to the Mahdi. I had a telegram from the Khedive asking me how it was he had to look for the news of his own province in an English paper (the *Times*), and why I could get news three days before his own Governor-General could telegraph it to him. I answered—I did not know, but that I went very much amongst the bazaars. The real answer is—the Governor-General is a Turk, who can't be made to see that three days, or for the matter of that three weeks, makes any difference in doing anything, and whose motto is, "Never do to-day what you can put off till tomorrow, or eternity, if you can manage it." Sir E. Baring's telegrams are very civil; he tells me that the Council only know what is going on in the Soudan by my two wires a day to him (and thus to the Khedive), and three times already the Governor-General was severely censured, and asked why he did not send important items I dwelt upon. He is under notice to quit, and Hussa Khalifa is named his successor. Hussa Khalifa is Sheik of the Bishereens, and is the first native ever named Haikender, or Governor-General; he deserves it, as the man has spent his life fighting for the Khedive, and he is Sheik of thousands of men, who would all feel any honour done him as done to themselves; also the post dromedary and telegraph wire pass solely through their territory till it strikes the railway at Assiout. I'm glad the present Governor-General is leaving, as he hates me, and I'm sure would do me any ill turn he could. You would be surprised how much influence being British Consul and *Times* correspondent gives me here. The people here have a very high opinion of the power of the *Times*. They say " that it was not Europe but the *Times* deposed Ismail Pacha " (and in this they are *au fond* right), and say " if this paper can change one Khedive, why not another ?" However, I've spoken enough about myself.

* * * * *

By-the-way, the Shakespeare M—— sent me has not yet arrived; some Arab student of English is now dog-earing it in his endeavour to distinguish a " hawk " from a " heron-shaw " in it.

Thursday, 27th.

The post has just come in, but no letters for

me. Colonel de Coëtlogan has just got the *Times*, with a misprint in it: "Colonel de Coëtlogan is assisting Pacha Power." This is such an extraordinary mistake that I'm afraid you will have doubts that I am the Power here in Khartoum. I hope it gave you no alarm.

Saturday, 29th.

No further news to add. No word of the relief from Cairo; however, if we go, Cairo and its worthless pack of Pachas will go too. A black lay sister of the convent at El Obeid escaped and came in yesterday; she came on foot by herself, and did the journey in twenty-two days. The only living European there, except the nuns and priests, was Baron Stheckendorff's German servant. The two we thought were prisoners were dead. She said the Mahdi was mustering his army to attack us; he has happily no ammunition for the Krupp battery—it was fired out by the Egyptians before they were killed. To-day is very bright and cold, a gentle breeze, but not a ripple on the river. I am busy now on a pen-and-ink drawing, "Benvenuto Cellini in his Atelier." I'll have it in time for the R.H.A. exhibition. . . . .

FRANK POWER.

KHARTOUM,
New Year's Day, 1884.

MY DEAREST MARY,

I got your very kind letter yesterday and newspaper, and was indeed sorry that my position here should have caused such grave anxiety at home. I knew you were aware I was not with Hicks, but, to reassure you, I purposely put into my telegram to the *Times* a list of those Europeans who were, and stated that de Coëtlogan and myself were the only Englishmen alive in the Soudan. I wired to Merrion Square yesterday to reassure you all. I will ask Sir E. Baring to forward the letter that was sent to Cairo for me. He appears to be a very kind man. I never saw him, and only knew him by telegraphing the situation to him; yet, on Christmas Eve, I got a telegram: " Baring—Cairo (private). Am sending by this post a few good English pipes and a case of English tobacco as a Christmas box to you." This was very civil to think of such a thing—he must now have so much to do, and such great responsibility. We have heard that the Mahdi is about to swoop down upon us; but we are now nearly able for him. In a few days, when the ditch is finished, and the Koneh and Duem garrisons in, we need have very little fear of the result; as for expecting any help from Cairo, that's all in my eye. On Nov. 27 a message was sent to Colonel de Coëtlogan that Baker Pacha and army HAD LEFT Suez for Suakim, and that Zuberh Pacha, with his 6,000 Bedawis, was already off from Cairo by train. On the 2nd it was telegraphed that the armies were on the road, and would be here in a few weeks. It is twenty-two days from here to Cairo by the Assiout route (train), and no reliefs have arrived; but I see by a Cairo newspaper of the 8th that not a man has yet left Cairo, and this morning Colonel de Coëtlogan gets a telegram from the Khedive to say that " he believes he cannot get together a column to relieve us, so we must depend on the neighbouring Sheiks for assistance." This is really rich, as the Khedive knows very well that there is not a Sheik in the Soudan who would, or dare, help us; and the fact of our sending to a tribe for help would confess our weakness and bring it down on us like a hundred of bricks. To show how much the Khedive knows of the place, he telegraphs to Colonel de Coëtlogan to ask—are the gates closed? as if the place had walls. It is an open town, with garden, fields, &c., and not a bit of defence round it till Colonel de Coëtlogan commenced the ditch, and yet they try to hamper our movements by trying to command us from Cairo. The latest fad was to order us to send half our garrison to Berber—a place that is perfectly safe, and has as large a garrison as ours. In your last letter you gave me very little news, the whole letter being taken up with my own stupid affairs, so I've very little to answer.

I would like to see the *Pictorial World* that has published my sketches. I got a letter yesterday from the new editor, saying that the paper had changed hands, and that all my sketches, ranging from July to September, only arrived the day of the news of Hicks' defeat. That is the beauty of registering a letter: it makes it go much slower.

The new editor prays me to send everything I can, and to name my own figure, so I will send some by this post to them.

January 2, 1884.

I see that my plain-spoken wire to Baring (of course prompted by Colonel de Coëtlogan) has brought the Khedive to reason. Colonel de Coëtlogan has just had a private telegram from the Khedive telling him to do all the things suggested in the wire. To-morrow morning's *Times* will have a little more plain speaking from me. I have sent an eye-opener (about 5,000 words), letting the British public know the true state of affairs and what Cairo Pachas are like. If our lives are to be sacrificed, it will not be said that the people in Cairo were kept in ignorance of the state of affairs here. At 12 o'clock to-night Colonel de Coëtlogan and myself are about to pay an unexpected visit on foot round the fortifications, to catch any guard, that may be negligent, on the hop. We have paved the bottom of the ditch and side of the fortification with spear-heads, and have for 100 yards the ground in front strewn with iron "crows' feet," things that have three short spikes up however they are thrown, and then beyond, for 500 yards, broken bottles (you know the Mahdi's men are all in their bare feet); at intervals we have put tin biscuit-boxes full of powder, nails, and bullets, at two feet under ground, with electric wires to them, so Messieurs the rebels will have a *mauvais quart d'heure* before they get to the ditch.

4 o'clock Thursday morning.

The Colonel and myself, having got the countersign for the night, set off at 1 o'clock this morning for a six-mile walk—that is, round the fortifications and back; he with sword and revolver, I sword and Empress rifle, and accompanied by Hasabala Effendi, his interpreter, an enormously fat young man. We had four soldiers behind, and one ahead with his rifle slung, to permit of his carrying the lantern. I had many a good laugh *en route*. We found all the sentries on the parapet perfectly on the alert, but one of them was deaf and dumb and had sore eyes. The gate-guard and officers turned out all right and advanced to ask the word and reply, but that was the only time we were asked it in the whole four miles of fortifications. When a sentry would challenge I would say, "Rounds," and then the Colonel would tell Hasabala to ask if all was well; he'd say, "In the name of the great God, is all good?" The sentry would reply, "'Tis perfect," and then Hasabala would reply piously, "Thank the merciful God." The private carrying the lantern was apparently called Abdallah, and on one sentry calling out when the challenge was finished, "Who will I report as having passed?" the lantern soldier in rags gravely replied, "Say Abdallah Ali." I translated the request and the answer to Colonel de Coëtlogan, who was highly amused at the conceit of the fellow, and told him for the future to say, "De Coëtlogan Bey." In one of the batteries we could not find the officer in command, and all were asleep except one sentry; it will be reported to-morrow to Ibraham Pacha; no doubt the officer will be reduced to the ranks. These sudden descents on the fortifications will sharpen up the guards, no doubt.

Friday night.

The two first nights of the festival of the Prophet's birthday have passed off quietly. We'll have three or four nights more of it. The post is just going out.

* * * * *

FRANK POWER.

KHARTOUM,
January 12, 1884.

MY DEAREST MOTHER,

* * * * *

They have done nothing for us yet from Cairo. They are leaving it all to fate, and the rebels around us are growing stronger. I can only send a line, as I've been writing all day and must send by this post. I send you a photo of Hicks and the staff; it is the only one extant. I would like it to be kept.

* * * * *

FRANK POWER.

KHARTOUM,
January 18, 1884.

MY DEAR MOTHER,

I just send you a line to reassure you. The climate here at present is delightful, but very cold at night; in the morning and evening I have to wear a great-coat, and during the day a white linen suit, such is the transition from cold to heat. I am sorry you are nervous about me; you'll find I will turn up all right. The order is already given for a retreat on Berber, but it will take us months to evacuate this town. The rebels are very near us, but, please Heaven, we will be all safe.

Bohndorff, a Central African explorer, passed through this week; he has been five years with the Niam-Niam cannibals. He brought me news of poor Schuver's death. I made him stay four days, and, after his life in the interior, our fresh food was a luxury to him. He was a very nice fellow. This was his fifth expedition to the interior. I have to-day written a long letter to the *Times* about his travels and the dwarfs and cannibals of the Velle River; it will be in a day or two after you get this. Look out for it. I was sorry to hear of poor Mrs. D——'s death at Alexandria. I last saw her at your dance two years ago. So P—— has "stowed the swag;" it is well to give up everything you have for your country, and become a patriot-martyr for a little time in Kilmainham.

* * * * *

We will be here for months yet, and, as we retreat along the postal line, I can always have the post *en route*.

* * * * *

FRANK POWER.

Khartoum,
January 24, 1884.

My dearest Mother,

I got your welcome letter on Monday, and several English and Irish papers; but not a word of the Shakespeare. I've inquired about the latter frequently. A few days ago they cut the wire, and closed the postal route towards Cairo; but this morning we opened it up again, and mended the wire. I am so sorry you are anxious about me. It would be cowardly and shameful for me to leave Khartoum now in the face of the enemy, and because there is danger here; even for your sake I would not do it. I am only doing my duty, and what every poor unpaid soldier must do. Both the *Times* and the Government have given me leave to go if I wish. However, the order for a general retreat is given, and we shall march *together* to Berber. I hear that Chinese Gordon is coming up. They could not have a better man. He, though severe, was greatly loved during the five years he spent here. To-day we have had two excitements. A Greek merchant who has been a year prisoner in El Obeid escaped, and arrived to-day. He says the only survivor of the *whole* of Hicks' army is Baron Sheckendorff's servant, who went over to the Mahdi before the battle, and fought on his side. I found him a decent, brave fellow. Sheckendorff, who had a quick temper, must have given him some terrible provocation. He was a troop-sergeant of Uhlans, and had the Iron Cross for bravery. The Greek tells us that after the battle, as each Sheik was shown the dead body of Hicks, he was permitted, in his turn, to plunge his spear into it; it is a custom they have, so that they may say they assisted at his death. My informant further states that the rebels only lost 300 men, as they kept behind rocks and trees till the army was almost annihilated by their shot and shell. Then they charged and killed the staff. The Mahdi has in El Obeid 35,000 regular soldiers whom he pays; those are independent of the tribesmen; and the Greek, who left Obeid thirteen days ago, says the army can march at an hour's notice. They have plenty of ammunition for the Krupp breech-loaders and for the Nordenfeldts, and fifty field-pieces. The priests and nuns and Greek merchants in Obeid are not interfered with, but are not permitted to leave the town. Just got a telegram from Mr. Bell, the *Times*' agent for Egypt, to say, " Gordon leaves Cairo to-night, and will be in Khartoum in eighteen days." The shortest time on record is twenty-four days; but Gordon (sword and Bible) travels like a whirlwind. No Arab of the desert could, when he was up here, vie with him in endurance on camel-back. Excitement No. 2.— The steamers *Abbas* and *Bourdain* came back to-day from a point on the Blue Nile between here and Sennaar. They were sent the day before yesterday to destroy a bridge of boats the rebels have made over the river near here, but they did not succeed. They were attacked with great fury by thousands of rebels, who killed some soldiers, but were beaten off themselves with great loss, but not until the two guns and rockets had fired eighty rounds of shell, and the men had blazed away till all was blue. They saw the bridge of boats, but could not get to it; so now all communication with unhappy Sennaar, by land or water, is cut off. The captains of the two steamers report that fifteen minutes from here the banks of the river are held by thousands of rebels with Remington rifles. The troops in Sennaar have not been paid for thirteen months, and the troops here for eight months. They are openly mutinous, and in rags. The Government has broken all its promises to them, and does not pay them, officers or men.

Sir E. Baring kindly sent me up two beautiful briar-and-amber pipes and a large tin case of tobacco, and Mr. Bell also sent me a briar-pipe by post as Christmas present; it was very thoughtful of both of them. Sir Evelyn Baring also wires me he will send me up a water-colour outfit. I send you his letter; he is a famous man, and you might like his autograph. I'll bring the girls home some beautiful native bangles. The native jewellers are wonderful workers. You buy the gold in dust, and pay for the workmanship. It is the purest virgin gold (24 carat).

* * ¶ * *

FRANK POWER.

KHARTOUM,
February 9, 1884.

MY DEAREST MOTHER,

Colonel de Coëtlogan says you greatly exaggerate what he has done for me (there he tells a whopper), but thanks you all the same for your kind wishes; he hopes to meet you, along with me, in " dear, dirty Dublin " before long. Get a triumphal arch stuck up somewhere near the square. One cab won't hold the two of us. We'll then leave for Barnum's Museum, New York! 'Tis from the nonsensical row some of the papers have made about us I build up my hopes of future Barnum fame, for really we have done nothing, only stuck here when every Egyptian who could run away bolted. I have a fine turkey, as big as Tom, my tame ostrich, fattening for the day Gordon comes next week. He and Colonel Stewart, 11th Hussars, will be tired when they arrive. We are going to give them roast turkey, a leg of mutton, Bass's pale ale, and lager beer. I will have Islamann on the top of the Palace to give the word to the cook when to put down the turkey; my telescope will spot the steamer ten miles down the Nile. I don't believe the fellows in Lucknow looked more anxiously for Colin Campbell than we look for Gordon. As regards relief of this place, when he comes he can only carry out the retreat. Sir E. Baring and Lord Granville seem to have the utmost confidence in me; it was solely on my confidential, and I hope conscientious, reports England has recognized the fact that the holding of Khartoum is *bosh*. I believe when Gordon comes he will sit upon me for this; but I have facts on my side, as also the turkey, &c., not to speak of the Bass and tobacco. We are all here in good humour to-day. A madman, a brother of Alideen Pacha, has arrived from

Cairo, and wishes to go up to Kashgate to pick his brother's bones out from those of Hicks and the rest of the staff. I have asked him if he has another brother to go prospecting after his bones in a few weeks; he is evidently an utter idiot. I am in very good health, barring five months of what has now become chronic dysentery. My eyes are rather troublesome, though I wear green glasses protected with close wire. The sun sets them on fire; they pain me very much even in the dark. I have to tie a cloth round them when I want to sleep at night. This is indeed "a land of desolation," as Baker called it. We must give it up. It has been plundered and robbed and "kourbashed" by the Egyptians, but, when we leave it, it will be scourged by slave-hunters. In the whole future of the Soudan I do not see a gleam of light through the blackness from which it takes its name. Here every one has small-pox. Near the market, where the "birit" Alamanine buys our food, there are four horses and a lot of camels dead for over five weeks, and their accompaniments of jackals and vultures. Smells are supreme. Colonel Coëtlogan and myself carry camphor to our nose all day. Until the rebels cut the wire this week, all my news was in type in London an hour after I had sent it from here; now there is no telegraph. If you get no further letters for a time, don't mind, as there are bands of rebels trying to cut off the posts ; only for that I would send the girls a lot of beautiful jewellery I have for them by registered parcel. Last week it would be safe, but to-day the "Postmaster-General for the Soudan," old Signor Ambrosio, tells me it would not be safe to send £57 worth of bangles. The work these native jewellers do is wonderful. The filigree is microscopic. I have several curios for you all; God grant you may ever see them or me. I have also got some of the beautiful native silk scarfs, worked with gold thread, fifty shades of different colours. One across one of the girls' white silk ball-gowns would look lovely. . . . .

I have no news to tell—only these little nothings.

* * * * *

FRANK POWER.

KHARTOUM,
February 14, 1884.

DEAREST MOTHER,

I'm afraid you have been anxious about me owing to the fact that up to yesterday the wire was cut, and we had no communication with the outer world. Now all is right, and you will see a despatch from me in to-morrow's *Times*. By looking at it each day you can be always assured of my safety. At midnight last night, the moment communication was established, I got the following telegram :—" From General Gordon, Berber, to Frank Power, British Consul. Best respects to you. I leave Berber to-day; will be in Khartoum on Sunday." We had been for days in great doubt about his movements, and I was besieged all day by people wishing to see the telegram and learn about the " Abu el Aswad ani," the father of the Soudanese. I was the only person he telegraphed to. He brings with him Colonel Stewart. There is no news here, except we've had a " Palace revolt," by which I was the principal sufferer. For the last month or so Colonel de Coëtlogan and I have been missing things—

shirts, stockings, and small things—but the other day I missed forty-four sovereigns, a bracelet, and twenty-four beautiful filigree silver coffee-cups. I had always kept my box locked. I said nothing, but that very evening I found a new key sticking in the padlock. The thief evidently forgot to take it out. I set to work quietly, and soon noticed that Alamanine (the cook), Ali, my boy, Islammann, the Colonel's boy (who was twice before forgiven theft), and the Colonel's tyce, or groom, were all in the swim, going up every day to the bazaar together spending money, &c. My kitchen is on the other side of the large court-yard, and on going down after midnight I found the four servants and *eight* soldiers of the guard making merry. I came upon them like a torpedo or bomb-shell, particularly as I had my lantern in one hand and a kourbash in the other. The servants are supposed to be in bed at 9 o'clock, but here they were gaily burning four of my candles (fearfully expensive here, and nearly all run out), a huge fire, about a stone of English potatoes, and a large pot of hot coffee with any amount of sugar in it. These latter were also mine, and, like all European produce, are **very** dear here owing **to the** route being half a year closed; only the wealthiest people can afford candles, coffee, or sugar. You should have seen their faces; the soldiers were away from their posts, and had no right to be there at all. The next day we sacked the four servants and brought them before the Pacha; they all denied the thefts, contradicted themselves, &c., and the Pacha had at once recourse to Egyptian justice, and wished to flog them till they confessed; such a flogging (as he admitted) means almost certain death. Of course I would not let them be touched; then he sentenced them to imprisonment for LIFE, and said "once he had them in prison they could be flogged," so I insisted that **they** should be set at liberty, as we had **no** conclusive **proof** against them. This rather puzzled these scoundrelly Beys and Pachas, and I had to threaten to report them to Cairo before I could be sure **the** poor wretches would be left unharmed. I asked how could they know any better than to steal when they saw Pacha after Pacha openly rob day after day, so I've had very little satisfaction **for** my loss, about £60, and I don't yet know how much more, and I've had the fearful bother to commence again teaching a pack of ignorant niggers that tumblers are not to be dropped on the ground, that I do not wish my spoons and knives cleaned by their being licked with the tongue, that I have no taste for mincemeat or fowls stuffed with mincemeat. (Forced meat is made by the young lady who for £2 a month deigns to officiate as our cook, chewing the meat till it is of the necessary fineness; I wondered at first how they chopped it so fine). You also have to teach them that Europeans do not like their servants to be rubbed all over with crocodile musk—a fearfully powerful *perfume*, and in great demand in the Soudan; one sniff acts as powerfully as a choppy day in the Channel or a dose of mustard and water. On all sides of us here are large armies of rebels waiting the word of the Mahdi, and the fools are letting the time pass; they could have had the town for the asking a month ago. I hope Gordon will be a nice fellow. We will be living together, &c., and I hope I will get on with him. It was civil to telegraph to me from Berber. I enclose the telegram; you may think it a curiosity. There was an autograph letter of the Mahdi seized here yesterday; if I can get it I will send it you. I hope I will be able to bring home my collection of weapons and skins. If so, you can make your hall a perfect museum. I've many beautiful native swords and suits of chain-mail, helmets, &c., all copied exactly from those of the time of Cœur de Lion. The fashion has been handed down from generation to generation. I have, amongst fifty other things, a Bari Sheik's war horn and drum; the horn is an *entire* elephant's tusk of beautifully fine ivory, hollowed out to an egg-shell thinness. This must have been the work of years. The drum is a large flat block of ironwood hollowed out by dint of labour; it is hung on a tree near the chief's hut, and the slightest touch is sufficient to make it actually roar or boom, so that it can be heard a great way off. I have a great collection of Shillook, Niam-Niam, Dinka, and Kordofan pipes, knives, shields, spears, poisoned arrows, and utensils. These cost me almost nothing. I am great friends with the native merchants in the bazaars, who do not care for these things, and, when they come across a curiosity, " Oh da wahad antika, sheel " uh; gie fie Hodafa Konsul el Ingleeze"—"Oh that's a curiosity; take it down to Sir Consul English." Some of these merchants, who sit all day in their little stalls in the bazaar, are really millionaires, and would buy up many of the London merchant princes. They live like kings in what, outside, looks like a mud hut. (If one shows any outward signs of wealth, the Pacha lets him know quietly that he will at once be charged as a rebel or something, and put in prison if he does not make him a little present, generally from £300 to £1,000.) G—— Pacha left here last year, admitting, report says, that in three years he had made £60,000; he came here three years ago as a clerk at £2 a month. Abdul-Kereem Pacha, the Governor, took a fancy to him, and made him chief of the tax-gatherers; in three years he gained the rank of Pacha and £60,000—meaning 5,000 ruined homes, several million strokes of the bastinado, rapine, robbery, and men driven to exasperation and shot down at their doors, the Khedowi declaring that for three years the Soudan had not been a source of wealth, but of poverty, to Egypt, but they forgot that in those three years it was the making of the fortune of several ex-slaves Pachas, &c.

Last evening we dined with a young merchant —— Effendi, a man who casually regrets the war because he has £15,000 worth of ivory at one of his stations on the White Nile, and he said, "I'll lose some money if the war spreads towards Abyssinia." Why? "At this time each year I get 5,000 camel-loads of gum, coffee, tobacco, and cotton from the district between Tredereff and Gondar in Abyssinia." He is a very handsome man, about twenty-five years old, and carefully dresses in Arab costume, and detests French boots, &c., affected by others. He always goes in for half-tones, I notice. Last night he had a long flowing robe of salmon-coloured silk edged with silver over an inner robe of black satin with a bronze silk sash, and wound round his head and shoulders a Shawal* or Kaifica of pale pearl or French gray edged with silver, crimson shoes, and a silver-mounted sword with precious stones in the hilt. He, of course, came and called

* Our word shawl and coiffeur come from Shawal and Kaifica.

for us, to escort us (about a mile) to his house, with twelve servants and some lanterns. On passing in, through a rickety gate in a high mud wall, we came on a court beautifully paved with coloured tiles, and the usual hosts of tame deer and gazelles about. No stranger can go into a Moslem's house proper—his hareem; so we were shown into the *salamlik*, or stranger's house, on the opposite side of the court. This is a large room, beautifully furnished with Persian carpets and divans, and two bed rooms off it, in case his visitors should like to stop the night. —— is a strict Mahometan, and does not drink wine; but he had for us Hennessy's . . . . Bass's pale ale, and Giessler's extra superior. These were all served with dates and raisins before dinner. Then six slaves (one of them a great curiosity here—he is quite a giant, and has a white patch on his face) carried in a silver tray, about six feet across, and put it down on trestles—the Arabs don't use tables. —— told us that when he asked us to dine he remembered we did not eat with our fingers, so that he had silver knives, spoons, and forks provided for us, and asked us to keep them as souvenirs.

Then followed the interminable thirty Arab dishes; the lamb roasted whole, the turkeys stuffed with pistachio nuts or truffles, the jellies and crêmes flavoured with lavender. Hasabala, the Colonel's interpreter, as usual, ate too much, and fell asleep; so I had to do the interpreter's work. We got home at twelve o'clock, to find Gordon's telegram awaiting me. By the way, the Government a year ago borrowed £12,000 from this Arab to pay the troops, and he has heard nothing of it since.

The Soudani and the Arabs are splendid fellows; ground down and robbed by every ruffian who has money enough (ill-gotten) to buy himself a position of Pacha, or free licence to rob, they are quite right to rebel and hurl the nest of robbers to the other side of Siout. For years it has been *kourbash, kourbash, et toujours kourbash*. This gets monotonous, and the poor devils rebel. I will, indeed, forgive the fellow who puts his lance into me, if that is to be my fate, because I will feel that he is right as long as I am of the same colour as the scoundrels who have robbed him and his for so many years. How is the government of the country carried on? It is only the plains along the banks of the Nile which are cultivated. Every Arab must pay a tax—for himself, children, and wife or wives. This he has to pay three times over—once for the Kedowi, once for the tax-collector or local Beys, and once for the Governor-General. The last two are illegal, but still scrupulously collected to the piastre. To pay this he must grow some corn, and for the privilege of growing corn he must pay £3 per annum. To grow corn the desert earth must have water: the means of irrigation is a "sakeh," a wheel like a mill-wheel with buckets on it, which raise the water into a trough, and then it flows in little streams over the land. A sakeh is turned by two oxen. Every man who uses a sakeh must pay £7 : if he doesn't use it, he must go into prison for life, and have his hut burned. Every one must pay for the right of working to earn money; every one must pay if they are idle; in any case every one must pay to make the officials rich. If you have a merkeb, or trading-boat, you are fined £4 if you don't continually fly the Egyptian flag and you must pay £4 for the privilege of flying it. It is this system, and not the Mahdi, that has brought about this rebellion. The rebels are in the right, and God and chance seem to be fighting for them, and, as long as I live to see you once more, I hope they will hunt every Egyptian neck and crop out of the Soudan. Better a thousand times the barbarities of slavery than the detestable barbarities and crimes of the Egyptian rulers.

As I was writing ten minutes ago, at about 11·30 at night, most fearful cries of "Murder—Help—I did not do it!" brought me trembling out, sword in one hand, revolver in the other, and my new boy with my rifle. It was that accursed sentinel: this is the third night he has alarmed Colonel de Coëtlogan and myself. Like all Egyptian sentinels, he sleeps on "his sentry go" (leaving his rifle and bayonet against the wall), and, when he sleeps, it appears, so the sergeant says, he always dreams— the one dream—and yells out his hideous night-breaking war-cry. He is a nuisance; he will be sent out to the works to-morrow. We don't object to the sentinel (like all in the town) sleeping soundly; but he ought not to yell, howl, raise all one side of the town with the only one dream he has got in stock. This I find, at the end of the third night, gets monotonous. He calmly says, "'Tis

Allah sends that bad dream to him." I quietly reply, " 'Tis the Colonel will order to-morrow fifty stripes to all sentinels found asleep at their posts, and if he was not asleep Allah would not send the dream." He mildly answers, " God is great; God makes me sleep when I am on duty; I cannot help it. It is God that is great." What are you to do with fellows like this? From morning till night it's " El Han da illah Inshallah," or " Bishmillah," dragging God's name into everything they do; not meaning to take it in vain; for they are really religious, and leave everything in God's hands. Imagine seeing every man, morning and night, spend twenty minutes each time at his prayer, out in the open; their faces lit up with religious fervour, fearing no man's ridicule, and only ashamed when they do wrong, not when they speak to their God. They say, " If we do not speak to God before all men, he won't speak to us when all men are gathered together to be judged." Do you remember this night two years ago? I've just been thinking of it. At this hour your ball was in full swing, and you had put me on fatigue duty, and I had brought poor Mrs. D—— down to supper. I did not think then that we would both be in Egypt together, and she taken in safe Alexandria, and I left scatheless in this hell upon earth, the Soudan. There are a great many of us dead since that night: poor Bailey, of the Queen's Bays; Mrs. D——, Mrs. C——, and Colonel C——, with whom I lunched that day. I suppose we all have our appointed time when we are to go, and the only thing is to be prepared for it. I write to R—— often. I have made three attempts to send him a sovereign by registered letter, for some paper, pencils, ink, &c., he sent up, but each time the money went to enrich some postal clerk who has a fancy to registered letters.

Friday Morning, *Feb.* 15.

This morning a mine was sprung upon us at our breakfast-table. A despatch arrived from the Khedive appointing Colonel de Coëtlogan a Pacha, a General, doubling his screw, and making him Acting Governor-General of the entire Soudan, about 2,000 miles long. We have had a great time; all the sycophants in Khartoum hurrying to kiss his hand, &c. I am very glad; he is such a good fellow, and deserves all he can get. I have got a new boy—a regular yahoo, a wild man of the woods—for a butler, who at once broke one of my lamp globes, and said it was a djin, or wandering sheitan (devil), did it. Though of a cannibal tribe, he says he has never eaten man meat. He is very handsome, and **coal**-black. I will bring him home as a present to you, to hand round five-o'clock tea in an Arab **costume**. Those boys are really very quick to learn, and beautifully neat; a week makes one of them a tolerable servant.

Saturday, *Feb.* 16, 1884.

The town is posted up with placards saying that, by Gordon Pacha's orders, the taxes are reduced to half. Slavery is freely permitted, and the Mahdi is proclaimed KING of Kordofan. De C—— Pacha is hard at work night and day: he to-day signed over three hundred orders, &c. . . . . I have a slight touch of fever on me to-day, and am going to take some quinine. Two or three times a week we get touches of fever. . . . . I've little more to say to you, having meandered on through so many pages aimlessly.

* * * * *

FRANK POWER.

KHARTOUM,
February 22, 1884.

MY DEAREST MOTHER,

I got your most affectionate letter yesterday. I need not tell you how glad I was to hear from home. I get all your letters; so continue to write. Colonel de Coëtlogan is gone to-day, and Gordon is here, as you doubtless have seen in the papers. Gordon, Colonel Stewart, and I now mess and live together. General Gordon, by permission of Lord Granville and Sir E. Baring, has promised to confer the Order of the Osmanli on me, and the Second Order of the Medjidji; he has also promised to take me with him to the Congo when this business is finished. To-day Sir E. Baring telegraphed: "H.M. Government highly approve of your action in the Soudan, and the aid you have given to General Gordon on his arrival. Lord Granville has intimated his wish that I send you this telegram." Gordon is a most lovable character—quiet, mild, gentle, and strong; he is so humble too. The way he pats you on the shoulder when he says, "Look here, dear fellow, now what do you advise?" would make you love him.

When he goes out of doors there are always crowds of Arab men and women at the gate to kiss his feet, and twice to-day the furious women, wishing to lift his feet to kiss them, threw him over. He appears to like me, and already calls me Frank. He likes my going so much amongst the natives, for not to do so is a mortal sin in his eyes. I often speak of you to General Gordon; he says he must make your acquaintance before we go to the Congo; he would like a day in Dublin. He is Dictator here; the Mahdi has gone down before him, and to-day sent him a "salam," or message of welcome. It is wonderful that one man could have such an influence on 200,000 people. Numbers of women flock here every day to ask him to touch their children to cure them; they call him the "Father and the Saviour of the Soudan." He has found me badly up in "Thomas à Kempis," which he reads every day, and has given me an "Imitation of Christ." He is indeed, I believe, the greatest and best man of this century. He asks me who I am writing to, and when I say "to you," he says he hopes you will some day give him a cup of tea, and like him. No one could help it. I stay on here to the end. I'll stop while he stays.

* * * * *

FRANK POWER.

KHARTOUM,
March 1, 1884.

MY DEAREST MOTHER,

You will, I know, excuse a short letter this week, when I tell you I have been nearly the whole week up the White Nile on a reconnaissance, and only returned this morning, and leave again at midday. I got a long letter from M—— on Monday (to-day is Saturday), and felt very thankful for all her prayers. Gordon says he hopes sincerely you will all pray for his success and join his name with mine. I enclose cheque to buy yourself some Easter present, as I cannot send you one. I like Gordon more and more every day; he has a most lovable manner and disposition, and is so kind to me. He is glad if you show the smallest desire to help him in his great trouble.

How one man could have dared to attempt his task, I wonder. One day of his work and bother would kill another man, yet he is so cheerful at breakfast, lunch, and dinner; but I know he suffers fearfully from low spirits. I hear him walking up and down his room all night (it is next to mine). It is only his great piety carries him through. He and I agree in a great many religious views. . . . . If at any time anything should happen to me in a reconnaissance, &c., General Gordon has a small box of mine to send home. You will find some jewellery in it, &c., for the girls, and some money which I will tell you about.

* * * * *

There is not the least fear now. All will go well, with God's help. . . . . I have lost several friends in Baker's defeat; but losing friends seem to be the rule in the Soudan. Excuse this hurried letter.

* * * * *

FRANK POWER.

KHARTOUM,
Friday, March 6, 1884.

MY DEAREST ANGELA,

I need not tell you how glad I was to get yours, Everard's, and Mary's letters on last Monday, particularly as your letter had, besides lots of news, your photo. I was also pleased to hear that Jack's ship had arrived safely. I am nearly sure I get all your letters, though sometimes late; for instance, I got a Christmas card from Mary on the 12th of January, and the Shakespeare never turned up. I get any amount of papers from mother and M——. Here the monotony is only broken by expeditions up and down the river, to let the rebels know there is a kick in us yet. Gordon is working wonders with his conciliatory policy. Of course, those French brutes must interfere. To-day a new French Consul, or a man entrusted with a secret mission from France, arrived here. There is not a French subject in Khartoum, or a penny's French interest in the Soudan since M. Marquet went from here, yet this fellow comes. He is the editor of the *Bosphore Egyptien,* a halfpenny evening paper in

Cairo, which was suppressed last week for violent attacks (personal and filthy) on Baring, Clifford-Lloyd, and the English officers, and horrible stories about our Queen. The people here, Greeks, Arabs, &c., all condemn the bad taste of the French in sending him here as Consul; he has not yet called on any of us in the Palace, but we three (Gordon, Stewart, and myself) are agreed as to how we will receive him. I had no firing on our expedition to the Blue Nile, although 3,000 men with rifles and cannon drew up to prevent our landing. They preserved a dignified silence. I send a book which Gordon gave me to M——. I know how much she admires him. He desires to be remembered to you all, and hopes you will continue to pray for his success. He has the greatest faith, he says, in women's prayers. I send you a present; you ought to get it two days after your birthday. I will send one to Fannie next mail. We will be out of this in about four months, when the General will go for three weeks to Brussels, to finish arrangements for the Congo; so I can be two weeks at home before I start with him across Africa (if I am spared as far, D.V.).

Last evening one of our steamers ran aground twelve miles from here, and as she was in danger Gordon sent me off with two steamers and strong hawsers to get her off. We worked all night (as the river is falling), and only got her off when we had taken everything out of her—fuel, chains, guns, &c. General Gordon was very pleased she was saved. Poor man, he is nearly worn out with hard work, but very cheerful.

* * * * *

FRANK POWER.

The letter of March 6, 1884, of which an extract has been given, was the last written communication we had from my brother. Thenceforth the only messages which came from him were his telegrams addressed to the *Times* as correspondent for that journal, and to Sir Evelyn Baring. Postal communication had been stopped.

His telegrams to the *Times* during the month of March and the beginning of April gave graphic descriptions of that portion of the siege. Their story is known to the world, and is too recent in men's minds to need repetition here. They told of the indomitable courage, the wondrous resource and generalship, the noble self-sacrifice, the reluctance to believe that he was abandoned, and the success in winning and keeping the loyalty of the people of Khartoum, which have marked Gordon as a great general, a true Christian, and a wondrous leader of men. But through all there ran the same note of warning of the near-approaching end; to all except the Ministry the same story was to be read, not only between the lines, but in express words—that provisions were running short, and that the time was nearing when the valour and determination of the defenders would avail no longer.

In those days, when telegrams were coming at uncertain intervals, " not containing," as a leading newspaper pointed out, " a single expression of despair," but yet clearly showing the danger that the devoted garrison stood in from day to day, more particularly in those sorties in which Colonel Stewart and my brother almost invariably took part, the anxiety felt at home was intense.

On April 9 my mother received a telegram from Sir Evelyn Baring, saying, "Gordon telegraphs to me Power is all right; he is a first-rate fellow." Then followed a message, published in the *Times* of April 17, descriptive of events in the siege up to a few days previous; and then—for nearly six months—silence!

On September 29 a telegram arrived, which I think should be given in full here. It ran as follows:—

"(BY EASTERN COMPANY'S CABLE.)

"KHARTOUM, *April* 28.
"(*Viâ* Kassala, Massowah, and Suakim.)

"Since my last telegram to you on April 21 we have been almost daily engaged with the rebels, who now thoroughly surround Khartoum. General Gordon is busily engaged laying out mines in front of the works in all directions. Yesterday and to-day the rebels came down to a village opposite and fired heavily on the Palace. We returned the fire with artillery and musketry, and on both occasions the Arabs soon retreated. There was no loss on our side. The town is quiet. Over half the population before the siege began went over to the rebels, thus weeding out all bad characters.

"General Gordon is issuing rations to the poor. Food is very dear. We have corn and biscuits for about four months. General Gordon has issued paper money, as our treasure is still at Berber. The merchants accept it as money, and all the arrears to the soldiers can be thus paid off. General Gordon has sent emissaries to offer to all the slaves of the rebels their freedom if they abandon their masters and come in. If they do this, it will be a fearful blow to the rebels. The General has hired the large Mission premises on the river, and has moved all the ammunition there; in case of attack with artillery on the fortifications, it will be perfectly safe.

"A messenger from Seyid Mahomet Osman, of Kassala, who is an Emir of Mecca and chief among the Mussulmans in the Soudan, has come in bringing a letter. The Seyid says he has beaten the rebels around Kassala, and he tells General Gordon to be of good heart and he and all his men will come to his relief. In such respect is this man held that the rebels did not dare to stop the bearer of the letter. One of General Hicks's bandsmen came in last night from El Obeid. The Mahdi has sent two guns, forty boxes of shells, and sixty Remingtons to be used against Saleh Bey, who is still holding out against the rebels at Mesalimieh. This soldier states that Slatten Bey, at Darfour, has not surrendered to the Mahdi. The Blue Nile is slowly rising, and we hope that in ten or fifteen days the steamers will be able to smite the rebels hip and thigh. The health of the town is excellent, and we three Englishmen here are well and hopeful. There are now around the lines, in addition to all other obstacles, such as crowsfeet, broken glass, wire entanglements, and *chevaux de frise*, three lines of land torpedoes or percussion mines. They are enormously powerful, and are much feared by the Arabs. We have no news whatever of the intentions of Her Majesty's Government. We learned to-day that a man with a post from Berber was taken by the rebels and killed.

"*July* 30.

"We have been now five months closely besieged, and can at best hold out but two months longer. The soldiers and people live in hopes of English relief, as since last May there are daily reports of English advancing from Dongola and Kassala. The Arabs have strong forts with cannon along the river, and they push the siege as vigorously as ever. General Gordon has protected all the steamers with bullet-proof plates of soft wood and iron, and on the six armoured barges has put up castles twenty feet high, giving a double line of fire. We have no fears of a rising in the town, as before the siege 8,000 to 10,000 men left and joined the rebels. The troops, to be loyal, must be paid, and General Gordon is badly off for money, none of that which left Cairo for his use ever having reached Khartoum. He has issued £50,000 worth of paper money. Food is daily distributed to the poor.

"Since March 23rd the following are the chief events of the siege:—

"March 23.—Hassan and Seyid Pachas were put to death for treachery in the battle of the 16th, in which we lost 350 killed and wounded.

"April 16, 17, 18, 19, and 20.—Attacks by the

rebels on the Palace from the villages opposite. Fearful loss of life to the Arabs from mines put down by General Gordon.

"April 27.—We heard of the surrender of Saleh Bey at Mesalimieh to the rebels with fifty shiploads of food, seventy boxes of cartridges, 2,020 rifles, and a steamer.

"May 1.—The officer commanding engineers, having put down a mine of 78 lb. of powder, trod on it, and with six soldiers was blown to pieces.

"May 3.—A man reported an English army at Berber.

"May 6.—Heavy attack from the Arabs at the Blue Nile end of the works; great loss of life from mines we had placed at Buri.

"May 7.—Great attack from a village opposite; nine mines were exploded there, and we afterwards heard that they killed 115 rebels. The Arabs kept up a fire all day. Colonel Stewart, with two splendidly directed shots from a Krupp 20-pounder at the Palace, drove them out of their principal position. During the night the Arabs loopholed the walls, but on the

9th we drove them out. They had held the place for three days.

"May 25.—Colonel Stewart, while working a mitrailleuse at the Palace, was wounded by the rebel fire, but he is now quite well.

"May 26.—During an expedition up the White Nile, Saati Bey put a shell into an Arab magazine. There was a great explosion, sixty shells going off.

"During May and June steamer expeditions were made daily under Saati Bey. Our loss was slight, and much cattle were captured.

"June 25.—Mr. Cuzzi, English Consul at Berber, who is with the rebels, came to our lines, and told us of the fall of Berber. Mr. Cuzzi has been sent to Kordofan.

"June 30.—Saati Bey captured forty ardebs of corn from the rebels, and killed 200 of them.

"July 10.—Saati Bey, having burnt Kalakla and three villages, attacked Gatarneb, but, with three of his officers, was killed. Colonel Stewart had a narrow escape. Saati's loss is serious.

"July 29.—We beat the rebels out of Buri, on the Blue Nile, killing numbers of them and capturing munitions and eighty rifles. The steamers advanced to El Efan, clearing thirteen rebel forts and breaking two cannon. Since the siege began our loss has been under 700 killed.

"*July* 31.

"This is the end of the fifth month of the siege. Yesterday I sent you *viâ* Kassala a despatch giving the situation here and the chief incidents of the siege since March 23. I wrote you several times each week up to April 23, when all hopes of men getting through to Berber had ceased. For the last five months the siege has been very close, the Arab bullets from all sides being able to fall into the Palace.

"Since March 17 no day has passed without firing, yet our losses in all at the very outside are not 700 killed. We have had a good many wounded, but as a rule the wounds are slight. Since the siege General Gordon has caused biscuit and corn to be distributed to the poor, and up to this time there has been no case of any one seriously wanting food. Everything has gone up about 3,000 per cent. in price, and meat is, when you can get it, 8s. or 9s. an ober. The classes who cannot accept relief suffer most.

"Since the despatch which arrived the day before yesterday all hope of relief by our Government is at an end, so when our provisions, which we have at a stretch for two months, are eaten we must fall, nor is there any chance, with the soldiers we have, and the great crowd of women, children, &c., of our being able to cut our way through the Arabs. We have not steamers for all, and it is only from the steamers we can meet the rebels.

"One Arab horseman is enough to put 200 of the bulk of our men to flight. The day Saati Bey was killed eight men with spears charged 200 of our men armed with Remingtons. The soldiers fled at once, leaving Saati and his Vakeel to be killed. A black officer cut down three of the Arabs, and the other five chased our men. A horseman coming up rode through the flying mass, cutting down seven. Colonel Stewart, who was unarmed, got off by a fluke, the Arabs not having seen him. With such men as these we can do nothing. The Negroes are the only men we can depend upon.

"The attack made by the Soudani troops under Mehemet Ali Pacha, on the 28th of this month, was most successful; the Arab loss must have been very heavy. As General Gordon has forbidden the soldiers to bring in the heads of rebels they kill, **it is** now hard to know **the** exact number. We captured that day sixteen shells and **cartouches** for mountain gun, a quantity of rifle ammunition, seventy-eight Remingtons, a number of elephant and other rifles, nearly 200 lances, sixty swords, **and** some horses. **Our loss** was four killed and some slightly wounded. This action **has cleared** away **the rebels, who day and** night have been firing **into our** lines **at Buri, on the** Blue Nile.

"The following day (29th inst.) a flotilla of five armoured steamers and four armoured barges with castles on them went up to Gareff, on the Blue Nile. I went with **them. On the** way up we cleared thirteen small forts, but at **Gareff** found two large strong forts—earthworks rivetted with trunks of palm-trees. There were two cannons in one. For eight hours we engaged these forts, and with the Krupp 20-pounder disabled their two cannons. The Arab fire was terrific, but, owing to the bullet-proof armour on all the vessels, our loss was only three killed and twelve or thirteen wounded. Towards the evening we drove the rebels, who were in great numbers, out of the forts.

"In three days General Gordon will send two steamers towards Sennaar. It is hoped they will retake the steamer *Mehemet Ali*, which the rebels took from Saleh Bey. General Gordon is quite well, and Colonel Stewart has quite recovered from his wound. I am quite well and happy."

The above message is the last complete account given, or which will probably ever be given, of the siege of Khartoum, unless the diaries of General Gordon, which are said to have been recovered, are brought down to a later date, or the papers of Colonel Stewart and my brother are found at Berber, where they are now reported to be.

The telegram was read everywhere with interest, and discussed and commented on in every newspaper in the kingdom. The *Times* of the same date commenced its leading article as follows :—

"We publish to-day a series of letters from our correspondent at Khartoum, which no Englishman will read without a thrill of pride and a flush of shame. They tell a story of unflinching courage, of unwavering fortitude, of inexhaustible energy and resource, of hope in circumstances of despair, and of splendid devotion to duty when hope had fled. In the long roll of Englishmen who have spent themselves in the service of England there is no brighter name than that won for himself by General Gordon, nor in the glorious catalogue of their exploits is there any that can outshine his defence of Khartoum. . . . . Others have faced frightful odds with the inspiring consciousness of generous sympathy at home seeking every means of affording them succour, but these three Englishmen at Khartoum, though happily spared the knowledge of much mean and bitter detraction, have fought under the chilling influence of growing indifference and final desertion on the part of those whose first duty was their relief. . . . When the curtain falls on the last day of July, we see the three Englishmen, knowing that their days are numbered, unless the unforeseen and the improbable comes to pass, setting their backs to the wall and facing their hard fate without a thought of flinching, and even without abatement of their cheerfulness."

There had come previously in the early part of September a report, unhappily unfounded, that a successful and decisive battle had been fought and the siege raised. A hope had grown up in England that this was so; but, alas! the true facts were far otherwise; and, on the day that my brother's last message was published to the world, its writer and Stewart had been betrayed and murdered by the Monassir Arabs, and Gordon, with Omdurman invested, was more closely besieged than ever, and more surely marked for destruction, in Khartoum—alone!

"Who can imagine," says a writer in the *Pall Mall Gazette*, "the gloomy thoughts that must have filled the minds of the three Englishmen as they stood alone beneath the sultry sun and confronted month after month the pitiless hail of shot which never failed for a single day?" But who can imagine, I ask, their thoughts and feelings on September 10 last, when the moment came when the three—nearer grown to one another than brothers —clasped hands in a last farewell? Telegrams had been sent with no avail; letters with no avail; solemn despatches, proclaiming their need, and still with no avail!

They had said everything of their danger that brave men could say and still be brave; but politicians "saw no reason to apprehend that Khartoum stood in need of relief." And so the time came at last when the three should part: when General Gordon decided to send on Colonel Stewart and my brother to cut through to the English lines if possible, and to tell in person the true state of the case—to sue for relief, not for himself, but for those whose safety he had pledged himself to take care of.

On September 10, entrusted with this mission, Colonel Stewart and my brother embarked on the ill-fated *Abbas*, and steamed down the Nile to Berber—and to death.

The stoker of the steamer tells the melancholy sequel in the following words:—

"The steamer *Abbas* left Khartoum about six months ago, with Colonel Stewart, two European Consuls, twelve Greeks, and several natives on board. Two other steamers accompanied her beyond Berber, and four nuggars sailed with us, which were towed as far as Berber by these two steamers. We shelled the forts at Berber, and our steamer having safely passed them, the others returned, we proceeding with the nuggars, which we also left behind before reaching Abu Hamad.

"On September 18 the steamer struck on a rock near a small island in the Wad Gamr country. We had previously seen many of the people running away to the hills on both banks of the river. Everything was landed on the island by means of a small boat. Colonel Stewart drove a nail into the steamer's gun, filed off the projecting end, and then threw the gun and its ammunition overboard.

"Meanwhile, several people came down to the bank shouting, 'Give us peace and grain.' We told them we had brought peace. Suleiman Wad Gamr, living in a house on the bank of the river, being asked for camels to take the party to Merawi, said that he would provide them, and invited Colonel Stewart and the two Consuls to the house of a blind man, named Fakrietman, telling them to come unarmed, lest the people should be frightened. The camels were not given us. We all went unarmed, except Colonel Stewart, who had a small revolver in his belt.

"Presently I saw Suleiman come out and make a sign to the people standing about the village, armed with swords and spears. These immediately divided into two parties, one running to the house of the blind man, the other to where the rest of Colonel Stewart's party were assembled. I was with the latter. When the natives charged we threw ourselves into the river. The natives fired and killed many of us, and others were drowned.

"I landed on a small island, and remained there until it was dark, when I swam over to the left bank. After some time I made my way to Hamdab, where I was seized, and taken to Sheikh Omar, Suleiman's uncle, at Birteh. I have been at Birteh ever since, and remained there when the dervishes ran away the day before yesterday.

" I heard that when the natives entered Fakrietman's house they fell upon Colonel Stewart and the Consuls, and killed all three. Hassan Bey held the blind man in front of him, thus escaping with a knife-wound only, and he afterwards went to Berber. Two artillery soldiers, two boat captains, and three of the native crew of the steamer are alive in Berber. A few slaves are also alive near Birteh. The money found was divided among the natives who murdered the party, everything else being sent to Berber. The bodies were thrown into the river."

A. P.

www.ingramcontent.com/pod-product-compliance
Lightning Source LLC
Chambersburg PA
CBHW031355160426
43196CB00007B/823